Eduardo

The Sy

A new version by Mike Poulton

Eduardo De Filippo (1900–84) was born in Naples into a well-known family of actors. He pursued acting himself, and in 1931 founded a theatre company in Naples with his brother Peppino and sister Titina, which performed a number of one-act plays written by Eduardo and Peppino. The company successfully toured Italy in 1933 and 1934, and also made a number of films beginning with *Three Men in Tails* (1932). In 1937 Eduardo attracted attention as a writer with his first screenplay, *I Did It*.

After the war Eduardo began producing his own works, including *Napoli Milionaria* (1945), *Too Many Ghosts!* (1946) and *Filumena Marturano* (1946), firmly establishing his reputation as a playwright; he produced more than fifty plays in his lifetime. In 1951 he published a highly acclaimed volume of poetry, *Naples, the Country of Pulcinella*, and in 1954 he reopened the celebrated Teatro San Ferdinando of Naples.

Saturday, Sunday, Monday (1959) was the first of his plays to receive an English production, at the National Theatre, London in 1973, with Laurence Olivier, Joan Plowright and Frank Finlay heading the cast.

Mike Poulton began writing for the theatre in 1995. His first two productions, *Uncle Vanya* and *Fortune's Fool*, were staged the following year at the Chichester Festival Theatre. Since then, productions of his work have included *Uncle Vanya* (Brooks Atkinson Theatre, New York, 2000); an adaptation of Turgenev's *Fortune's Fool* (The Music Box, New York,

2003), which received a Tony nomination for Best Play and went on to win seven major awards; Schiller's *Don Carlos* (The Crucible, Sheffield, 2004/Gielgud Theatre, London 2005); *The Canterbury Tales* (RSC, international tour, 2005/ Gielgud Theatre, 2006); *The Father* (Minerva Theatre, Chichester, 2006); *The Cherry Orchard* (Clwyd Theatr Cymru, 2007); *The Lady from the Sea* (Birmingham Rep, 2008); Schiller's *Wallenstein* (Chichester, 2009); and Schiller's *Mary Stuart* (Clwyd Theatr Cymru, 2009).

His more recent work includes *Anjin* (Tokyo and Osaka, 2010); *Morte d'Arthur* (RSC, Stratford-upon-Avon, 2010); *The Bacchae* (Royal Exchange, Manchester, 2010); and a new version of Schiller's *Luise Miller* (Donmar, 2011).

Eduardo de Filippo

The Syndicate

A new translation of
Il sindaco del rione Sanità
by
Mike Poulton

Methuen Drama

Published by Methuen Drama 2011

Methuen Drama, an imprint of Bloomsbury Publishing Plc

1 3 5 7 9 10 8 6 4 2

Methuen Drama
Bloomsbury Publishing Plc
36 Soho Square
London W1D 3QY
www.methuendrama.com

ISBN: 978 1 408 15690 2

Available in the USA from Bloomsbury Academic & Professional, 175 Fifth
Avenue/3rd Floor, New York, NY 10010. www.BloomsburyAcademicUSA.com

A CIP catalogue record for this book is available from the British Library

Typeset by Mark Heslington Ltd, Scarborough, North Yorkshire
Printed and bound in Great Britain by CPI Antony Rowe, Chippenham and Eastbourne

The Syndicate

Synopsis

Honest young Antonio Barracano had stabbed a brutal nightwatchman to death. With the help of an American-Italian 'Godfather' he had been smuggled out of Naples to hide in New York. In his absence Antonio had been convicted of the murder. Safe in New York, working for his rescuer's 'family', the young man had quickly acquired wealth and a reputation for ruthlessness. After several years he'd returned to Naples and used his wealth and reputation to quash his original murder conviction and to set up as a shady property developer. Soon he is feared and respected all over Naples. But with the help of his friend Doctor Fabio Della Ragione – whom like everybody else he terrorises – he decides to make it his life's work to provide a form of rough justice for the criminals of the city who have no other access to law. Don Antonio knows that there's corruption in every aspect of Neapolitan officialdom and that the poor and the ignorant who don't know the system and can't afford the bribes would be lost without him. We see his eccentric form of justice in action. For thirty years he has ruled the Naples underworld with a rod of iron. But when a respectable but poor young man decides to murder his father and comes to Don Anto' for advice, the Neapolitan 'Godfather' decides to emerge from the shadows and take the young man's case. The comedy grows blacker as 'respectable' Naples collides with its criminal underworld.

Mike Poulton's translation of *The Syndicate* premiered at the Minerva Theatre, Chichester Festival Theatre, Chichester on 21 July 2011. The cast was as follows:

Don Antonio	Ian McKellen
Donna Armida	Cherie Lunghi
Geraldina/Vicenza	Margaret Clunie
Gennaro/Peppe	Philip Correia
Amedeo/Zibacchiello	Mark Edel-Hunt
Dr Fabio	Michael Pennington
Arturo Santaniello	Oliver Cotton
Rafiluccio Santaniello	Gavin Fowler
Rita	Annie Hemingway
Catiello/Luigi	David Shaw-Parker
Immacolata	Jane Bertish
Vicienzo Cuozzo	Brendan O'Hea
Palummiello	Michael Stevenson
Nait	Michael Thomson
Pascale Nasone	David Foxxe
Pascale's Wife	Janet Spencer Turner

Director Sean Mathias
Designer Angela Davies
Lighting Designer Tim Mitchell
Casting Director Gabrielle Dawes

Characters

Antonio Barracano (*Don Anto'*)
Armida (*Armi'*), *his wife*
Geraldina (*Dina*), *his daughter*
Gennaro (*Gennarino*), *his son*
Amedeo, *his son*
Dr Fabio Della Ragione, *Don Anto's right-hand man*
Arturo Santaniello, *owner of two prosperous pastry shops*
Rafiluccio Santaniello, *his son*
Rita, *an orphan engaged to Rafiluccio*
Catiello (*Catti*), *Don Anto's watchman in Terzigno*
Immacolata (*'Macula, 'Macolata*), *Don Anto's housekeeper in Terzigno*
Vicienzo Cuozzo, *a poor but honest man*
Palummiello, *a young small-time con man*
Nait, *a young crook*
Pascale Nasone, *a successful pimp and loan-shark*
Nasone's Wife, *a tart*
Peppe Ciucciu, *a thug*
Zibacchiello, *another thug*
Luigi, *Don Anto's caretaker in his Naples home*
Vicenza (*Vicenzella*), *his daughter*

Act One

*Time: mid-September 1960, 3.45 a.m. – just before dawn. A large,
comfortable sitting room. Through French windows which lead onto
a low balcony which gives access to the extensive grounds of the
house in Terzigno – endless olive groves and vineyards – we can see
the slopes of Vesuvius, the volcano itself in the distance and the Bay
of Naples.*

Immacolata, *the housekeeper, still half-asleep and yawning, is
putting on her dressing gown. A muffled intercom bell can be heard.
She is anxious to prevent it waking the household. She moves an
elaborate painting to reveal, in a niche, a bell and a speaking tube.
She pushes the bell and speaks into the speaking tube.*

Immacolata   Right – OK.

*She replaces the first picture and moves a second one, on another
wall. Behind this is an old-fashioned telephone. She speaks into it to*
Catiello *the watchman and caretaker.*

Immacolata   Catiello? You can open the gates.

*She lights a lamp and goes out to one of the other rooms where we
hear her knocking softly but urgently on a door. She comes back
then disappears to a distant part of the house where the knocking
process is repeated.* **Geraldina**, *youngest of* **Antonio**'s *children,
comes on, in her dressing gown, trying to wake herself up. She is
attractive, aristocratic and focused on the task in hand. She pins
up her hair, takes a large white sheet out of a cupboard and from a
drawer something which we will later recognise as a surgical gown.
She spreads the sheet over the central table and the gown over a
chair.* **Gennaro** *enters, unkempt, in his pyjamas. He's twenty-three,
elegant, handsome, half-asleep, not so well co-ordinated as his sister,*
Geraldina, *but he knows what is required of him. He has done this
so often that one feels he could carry out his tasks in his sleep. All
three improvise 'good mornings' and other waking-up conversation.
From a sideboard* **Gennaro** *takes a tin box of surgical instruments,
a chromium machine for sterilising the instruments, a spirit burner,
bottles of iodine, etc.* **Immacolata** *returns, bringing enamel basins,*

bandages, linen towels, cotton wool, etc. Conversation stops. Swiftly and with great precision all three convert the sitting room into an operating theatre. Kitchen chairs are brought to use as trestles. Two planks are used as an operating table over which the women spread a sheet. **Gennaro** *brings a floor-standing, electric reading lamp which he positions over the operating table.* **Doctor Fabio Della Ragione** *enters in his dressing gown and pyjamas. He's a likeable, intelligent cynic but at the moment he's a little out of temper at having been woken so early – but his grumpiness is not directed at his three helpers whom he greets gruffly. He checks to see everything is in order.* **Immacolata** *helps him off with his dressing gown and on with his surgical gown,* **Geraldina** *pours surgical spirit into the basin.* **Gennaro** *puts the instruments into the basin.* **Immacolata** *ignites the spirit which flares up. The flames cast unearthly shadows on the walls of the room.*

We begin to hear the muffled sounds of **Nait** *and* **Catiello** *helping* **Palummiello** *down the corridor towards the room.* **Palummiello** *has been shot in the leg and is in great pain. He and* **Nait** *are young, petty criminals and the best of friends but* **Nait** *is responsible for the shooting. The harsh things to say to and about each other in the scene is at odds with their physical closeness, support and concern for each other. The audience should get the feeling that without each other either one would be helpless.* **Catiello** *is an unflappable old family retainer in late middle age. He's seen it all before. The three men improvise grunts, cries of pain and words of encouragement over and above what is in the script.*

Offstage.

Palummiello   Ah! Jesus! . . . Jeez . . .

Catiello   Hey! – Keep the noise down! Shhh! We've almost made it.

Palummiello   Holy Mother of God . . . I just can't . . . go another . . .

Nait   You're doing fine

Catiello   C'mon, come on . . . Call yourself a man? Careful!

Palummiello   I'll have to stop – just give me a minute.

All three rest.

Catiello   You don't have a minute . . . I'm not your nurse. And you're –

Nait   He'll get gangrene in it if he doesn't hurry up –

Catiello   keeping the doctor waiting –

Palummiello   Oh Jesus . . . Jesus . . .

Painfully, they get him moving again.

Catiello   Think about something else – anything. Concentrate –

They appear in the doorway.

Nait   Try singing. Sing something –

Palummiello   I don't feel like singing – Ah! Jesus!

Finally they enter. **Palummiello** *is placed on the operating table. The operation that is about to take place is conducted with the utmost skill and efficiency by all concerned.* **Nait** *holds* **Palummiello***'s head and shoulders and supports him throughout.* **Immacolata** *closes the shutters of the French windows,* **Gennaro** *switches on the electric lamp. It's dazzlingly bright – clearly now, not a reading lamp.* **Geraldina** *helps* **Fabio** *on with his rubber gloves.* **Immacolata** *goes out to the kitchen.*

Fabio   And you are?

Nait   Nait. I shot him.

Fabio   Syringe.

He indicates a phial. **Geraldina** *loads the syringe.*

Palummiello (*screaming in pain*)   Ah! Holy Mother of God!

Fabio   Try to moderate your screams. Don Antonio's still asleep. (*To* **Nait**.) If it was you who shot him –

Nait   I did shoot him, sir –

Fabio (*accepts syringe from* **Geraldina**)   – why are you here?

Nait　Well . . . Because . . . It's a long story – I was at the end of via Marina around quarter to two – You know those crossroads? – there's a right turn to San Giovanni a Teduccio, and if you take a left you're on the motorway for Pompei –

Palummiello (*screams*)　Ah! You're killing me!

Fabio　Lower his trousers, Gennaro.

Gennaro *pulls down* **Palummiello**'s *trousers;* **Fabio** *skilfully administers the jab* **Palummiello** *flinches.*

Fabio　Give it a moment to work. Scissors, Geraldina.

Geraldina *uses the scissors to cut off* **Palummiello**'s *trouser leg. An ugly wound is exposed. The flame in the basin begins to die down.* **Fabio** *picks up the probes and instruments he will need with forceps.*

(*To* **Nait**.) Sorry. Go on.

Nait　We were shooting at each other – He fired too. With . . . (*Takes out a gun.*) This is his.

He shows the gun around as if he wants somebody to take it off his hands.

Fabio (*alert*)　Nobody touch it. Why are you trying to unload his gun on us? Keep it out of sight. Then what happened?

Nait *puts the pistol back in his pocket.*

Palummiello (*through teeth clenched in pain*)　I was bleeding, in need of help . . . He knew I'd been hit – He just ran for it . . . Bastard!

Nait　So I should have hung around and got myself arrested? I just started walking towards the station goods yard as if nothing had happened. Walking, walking, and in my head his yelling's getting louder: 'Help me! Somebody help me.' Then – Mother of God! We're friends aren't we? In the end I found a taxi – headed back there at full speed – I took him in my arms, I hauled him on board and I carried him here.

Palummiello   I took him for some innocent passer-by . . . That's why I didn't shoot him.

Nait   I couldn't leave him in the gutter not knowing what sort of a mess I'd made of him, could I?

Palummiello (*in pain, offers* **Nait** *his hand*)   Thanks.

Nait (*moved, he shakes hands energetically*)   I knew you'd understand; it had to be done. Now we must think about getting you better.

Palummiello   When I'm better I'll kill you.

Nait   You and whose army?

Fabio   Haven't you done enough! The slightest excuse and you start firing off at each other . . . The most trifling of reasons –

Nait   No, sir, you're wrong: the reasons are always deadly serious. You have to understand that he –

Fabio   Kindly leave me out of it. I just . . . don't want to know.

His comments on the shooting become a comment on the underworld of which **Nait** *and* **Palummiello** *are a part.*

Fabio   What a way to behave! 'Why don't I shoot you?' 'Fine! Why don't we all shoot each other!'

Immacolata *brings a tray of coffee; she serves the doctor, then the others.*

Palummiello (*pleading*)   Some water –

Fabio   No. No liquids.

Palummiello (*in pain*)   Ah! Jesus! Mary! –

Fabio   I've asked you not to scream like that. You're crying now? You should have thought of the pain before you started shooting.

Palummiello   Try telling that arsehole –

Nait   You're the arsehole.

Fabio (*sipping coffee*)   Fine. So you're both arseholes. The Stinking Arsehole Twins.

Nait   Don't you want to know what it was about?

Fabio   It's of no interest whatsoever. Basin!

They prepare the wound. The leg is now fully exposed. The area around the wound is cleaned with forceps and swabs of iodine. **Palummiello** *makes a great song and dance about it but obeys* **Fabio***'s warning and has stopped screaming out loud. The children act as assistants. They dip their hands in disinfectant and hold them up to let them dry.* **Fabio** *does the same.* **Gennaro** *helps* **Nait** *to hold* **Palummiello** *down. At moments of extreme pain* **Immacolata** *holds her hands over* **Palummiello***'s mouth. Finally with great skill* **Fabio** *prods about looking for the bullet – he finds it.*

Fabio   The handkerchief.

Immacolata *folds up a clean white handkerchief and stuffs it in* **Palummiello***'s mouth. In silence* **Fabio** *removes the bullet. Though from outside comes the sound of horses, the bells on their collars and their drivers singing folk songs as they go towards the market.* **Nait** *can't bear his friend's pain any longer and moves away from the operating table.* **Palummiello** *has fainted.* **Gennaro** *relaxes his grip then gets himself a coffee. They all relax.* **Immacolata** *opens the shutters and then the French windows. Dawn is now well on the way. Birds are singing.*

Nait (*anxious*)   How's he doing?

Fabio (*his reply is to show* **Nait** *the bullet*)   A thirty-eight. He'll live.

Nait (*genuinely grateful for the intervention, as he sees it, of Our Lady*)   A miraculous escape! He should take it to Pompei and offer it to Our Lady.

Fabio   Why? I should think she has more Neapolitan bullets than she knows what to do with – and every one a miraculous escape. Get him outside. He needs air – Immacola – put one of the chairs on the . . .

Gestures towards the balcony.

Throw a bedspread – a rug or something over him. When he comes round you can clear off.

They start to move him out.

Palummiello (*semi-conscious*)   But . . . I want to talk to Don Anto'.

Nait   Me too.

Immacolata (*protectively*)   Don Antonio's still asleep.

Gennaro   He needs to rest. The longer the better.

Fabio   Did he get any sleep last night?

Immacolata   A little. The fireworks tired him out.

Gennaro   What a display! Three masters of the pyrotechnic art trying to outdo each other: Turrese, Pachialone and the little fellow from Siberia.

Geraldina (*her eyes sparkle*)   Oh, Turrese was inspired!

Gennaro   But Pachialone was the best.

Geraldina   What? Rubbish! – he's not in the same league. The bombshells Turrese sent up were incredible – devastating – so high that just looking up at them made your neck ache – and then when they exploded into such beautiful shapes – a fan, a rose – perfectly formed – Ah! And just when you thought it was over another explosion, and another, more and more . . . then three or four specials – three earthshaking crashes that rattled the windows: I thought the whole house was going to collapse about our ears. Turrese – nobody comes near him.

Immacolata   I was watching all Turrese's friends sneaking looks at Don Antonio to see if his expression was giving anything away – but he just nodded his head like this – (*she demonstrates*) as if to say 'Well done, well done!'

Catiello   But when it came to Pachialone's turn – a chance to show what he was made of – Don Antonio's face gradually started to cloud over – and as for the little fellow from Siberia – he'd only set off two or three of his fireworks when – Well! – Don Antonio just said 'Goodnight' – nodded to his friends and went off to bed. Yes. He said 'Goodnight', but what he meant was: 'This is pathetic. It stinks.'

Immacolata   So naturally everybody else slipped off home too. As was only right. Respectful. It was nearly midnight anyway. After ten or fifteen minutes I went and opened his door, softly, very softly – I always do – and he was sleeping like a baby.

Fabio   My God! So nobody has told him about Donna Armida?

Immacolata   Like I said, he was already asleep when –

Fabio   How is she? Still no news?

Immacolata   She was rushed to casualty in Naples. They say she was lucky to get away with twelve stitches.

Fabio   It would have to happen last night – before I got back from town – Madness! I should have been here to dress your mother's wounds.

Gennaro   We drove her – Amedeo and I.

Fabio   And they kept her in?

Gennaro   No. But after the stitches Mamma was in a lot of pain – She couldn't face another car journey – not all the way back here. So Amedeo said best to take her to his place.

And then bringing her home so soon after it happened . . . well, there may have been a row, then Papa may have woken up and . . . it doesn't bear thinking about . . .

Immacolata   Amedeo phoned about three to say that Donna Armida was feeling a little better – she wasn't in so much pain.

Fabio   And Don Antonio – how many times do you have to tell the man! He loves those dogs – reared them from puppies – lets them slobber all over him. He refuses to see how dangerous they've become – The whole family's at risk! – we're talking about large, ferocious predators, loose in this . . . I'll bet it was Malavita. He's a gangster not a dog.

Immacolata   When he shows his teeth it's like looking into the jaws of Hell.

Gennaro   Well, whichever one it was is not long for this world – Malavita or Munaciello – one of them's going to get a bullet through the head. I'll see to that.

Geraldina   You? Shoot one of Papa's dogs? You wouldn't dare –

Gennaro   Oh? When he sees the state Mamma's in he'll get his revolver and blow its brains out himself.

Fabio   I should hope so too.

Immacolata   Poor Donna Armida! The guilty dog has had his ears tickled for the very last time.

Gennaro   I'll shower and get dressed; then I'll get the get the car and go into Naples – to the shop. Do me a couple of scrambled eggs and some coffee, Immacolata.

Immacolata   Right.

Gennaro   So, Doctor. If there's nothing –

Fabio   No. You get off. Fine.

Exit **Gennaro**.

Geraldina   I'll have coffee too. White.

Goes back into her room.

Immacolata   How about you, Doctor? Do you want anything? Coffee?

Fabio   Not finished this one. I'll wait until Don Antonio gets up – When you bring him his breakfast I'll have a glass of cold milk. Yes. I'll keep him company.

Immacolata   Shall I fetch you some biscuits?

Fabio   If you like.

Catiello   I'm off. Get something inside me. I think there's some pasta and beans from yesterday. So if that's all –

Fabio   Yes. Go and have your breakfast.

Catiello   Just ring if you need me.

Indicating the bell behind the painting.

Fabio   Yes, yes. How many this morning?

Catiello   There were to have been ten – all with appointments – but yesterday morning Don Antonio had me cancel seven of them. 'I've come to Terzigno for a holiday,' he says.

Fabio   Good for him. And in three weeks we'll . . . Well, *he'll* be back in the city. I . . .

Thinks better of pursuing it.

He never stops! What a life . . .

Catiello   It *is* his life. Half Naples grinds to a halt when he's away from it – even for a few days.

Fabio   Yes. And there are days when it's as if the other half of Naples is trying to shove its way through his front door.

Catiello   Anyway. Just the three this morning. Pascale Nasone's one of them.

Fabio Who?

Catiello He's a nobody – small change. And his petition –
he'll be in and out of here in minutes. It's just that once he
found out that Don Antonio had made it his business to look
into the affair – well, now Nasone can't keep his nose out of
it. Shouldn't be a problem though. He's been told to bring
his accuser with him: Vicienzo Cuozzo. They'll be made to
shake hands in front of Don Antonio and that'll be the end
of it. And the third is Arturo Santaniello's boy, Rafiluccio.

Fabio Who?

Catiello Arturo who has the pastry shop in via Giacinto
Albino – him with the dead wife. Anyway the boy was here
yesterday, and the day before, and in the end Don Anto' said
come back this morning. So you see the day's pretty free.

Fabio Good. I need to talk to him myself.

Catiello You letting them stay there? (*Gestures towards*
Palummiello *and* **Nait** *on the balcony.*)

Fabio Shut the doors. If they want to wait they can wait
outside.

Catiello Sure?

Fabio Yes, It'll be OK.

Catiello (*going out onto the balcony; to* **Nait**)   If you'll give me
a hand with your friend . . . A bit this way . . . He'll get the
morning sun . . .

*Together they move the wounded man and his chair further along the
balcony and out of sight. After a while* **Catiello** *comes back.*

I'm off.

Fabio Shut the doors.

Catiello *shuts the French windows onto the balcony.*

Immacolata (*coming in*)   He's awake.

Fabio   Surely not? It isn't six yet.

Immacolata   He gave three rings. One after the other. That means he's been up and about for nearly quarter of an hour. I must –

She goes quickly towards **Don Antonio**'s *room but, to her horror, he appears in the doorway; under her breath.*

Oh no! He's –

Fabio   S'been a hot night. Nobody could . . .

Antonio *is standing in the doorway. He brings with him an air of absolute authority. He wears expensive slippers and a dressing gown over his nightshirt. He's seventy-five, sunburnt, alert, healthy, fit and wiry. His eyes miss nothing, though for a lot of the time he seems to avoid looking directly at anything or anybody – in fact he keeps his eyes half-closed. When he chooses to stare at somebody the effect on the victim is icy and devastating. His manner of studied joviality hides a dangerous, terrifying inner life. In some ways he is like a caged, dangerous animal.* **Fabio** *jumps to his feet and greets* **Antonio** *with a slight bow.* **Immacolata** *retreats a few steps and manages a nervous smile.* **Fabio** *and* **Immacolata** *can't relax until they detect what sort of a mood* **Antonio** *is in this morning.* **Antonio** *nods in response to their respectful 'Good-morning, Don Antonio', then goes to the table and sits down. There is a long pause during which* **Antonio** *gives them no hint of his mood.* **Immacolata** *and* **Fabio** *exchange nervous glances. Then* **Antonio** *looks at* **Fabio**. *He points at a chair, indicating that* **Fabio** *may sit down.* **Fabio** *sits.*

Antonio (*massaging circulation back into one of his feet*)   You're up early this morning?

Fabio *and* **Immacolata** *don't know which of them is being addressed. This is deliberate on* **Antonio**'s *part. He slowly turns to study them.*

Antonio   She's always up early – eh, Immacolata? I was talking to you. Doctor.

Fabio   Oh, I see. To me . . .

Antonio   So?

Fabio   There's been a . . . slight disturbance.

Antonio (*not interested*)   Ah . . .

Fabio   Bullet wound. Nait and Palummiello . . . shooting at each other.

As if making a formal report.

They turned up here at about half-past four –

Immacolata   Quarter to. It was only a quarter to four . . .

Fabio   Well, anyway – What happened was –

Antonio (*silencing him with a gesture of his left hand and*)   Shhh! . . . Not now, Doctor . . . Later, later . . .

Fabio *covers his mouth with his right hand; with his left he gestures: 'Sorry. I'll not say another word.'*

Antonio   'Macula!

Immacolata   Yes, Don Antonio?

Antonio   Bring in the shameless one.

Immacolata (*nervous: hasn't a clue*)   Who? The shameless one . . .

Antonio   The enemy I can't silence.

Immacolata   Doctor . . . ?

Fabio *hasn't a clue either.*

Antonio   The only one in the world who, when he speaks, speaks the truth.

Fetch me the mirror, 'Macula – the mirror.

Immacolata   Ah! I was never any good at riddles.

She goes to get the mirror.

Antonio (*thinks for a moment*)   No, I'm mistaken. There's something else that never lies: Death, Doctor . . . Death.

Man's supremacy among wild beasts rests upon a unique talent for hypocrisy, evasion and lying. He'll sanction the most blatant injustices – simply by pretending to be deaf, dumb, blind, indisposed, sick of the palsy, barking mad . . . Or if it suits his purpose, he'll make you believe he's knocking at Death's door. Yes, it takes a good doctor – I'm looking at you, Doctor . . . to separate the sick man from the malingerer. You waste most of your life chasing after the truth of a man – until a time comes when the doctor can at last be certain of his prognosis. Finally he knows what's really in his patient's heart – no possibility of a mistake. The heart learns to speak the truth – it stops. Dead. Can't argue with that, eh? Doctor?

Fabio   Well . . . I suppose not.

Immacolata (*bringing the mirror*)   The 'enemy you can't silence'.

Antonio (*to the mirror*)   Hey! Have you no respect! Nobody speaks to me like that! So I'm seventy-five years old – Who's counting? What, this?

Running his finger along a furrow in his brow.

Well, it's nothing to do with my age. No, it has a name: Giacchino. Before he became a line on my face he was a watchman over at the Marvizzo place. Yes . . . You must remember? Giacchino . . .

Fabio   Better to let him rest in peace.

Antonio   He's been here – on my forehead since I was eighteen. And these . . .

Running his finger along other lines.

Each one a memory. Something. Someone. I tell you what, Doctor . . . You want to know what seventy-five years of age means? Watch. I make a little depression with my finger . . .

I take away the finger, the depression remains. Old flesh.
The dough of peasant bread. It takes a while before the
shape of the face . . . reasserts itself.

Fabio (*meaning it*)   Don Anto', you have nerves of steel and a
cast-iron constitution.

Antonio   Yes? Then we should set up as scrap-metal
merchants.

Gives the mirror back to **Immacolata**.

Antonio   Here, take it away! It's not always good to tell the
truth.

She puts it away.

'Macula!

Immacolata   Don Antonio?

Antonio   I want to get dressed.

Immacolata   Right. What about your shower?

Antonio   Had it.

Immacolata (*with a sense of having been outmanoeuvred*)   Oh?
Why didn't you call me?

Antonio   Wasn't necessary. Also . . . I needed to be alone. I
want to get dressed. No I don't – I want my breakfast. Then
I'll get dressed.

Immacolata   I'll fetch it.

Exit.

Antonio (*yawns*)   All these pills you fill me up with, Doctor –
and they produce only three hours sleep . . . Not enough. I
need five. Five hours sleep.

Fabio   In fact I prescribed only two tablets. One before
dinner. One after.

Antonio   I heard a car drive up to the gates – Catiello
talking – you all moving about out here. I knew what was

going on but I thought to myself: if they want me, they'll call me.

Fabio   There was no point in disturbing you. We had everything we needed.

Antonio   Geraldina assisted?

Fabio   Geraldina, Gennarino and Immacolata.

Antonio   And Amedeo?

Fabio   Amedeo? No.

Antonio   Oh? Why not?

Fabio   He drove back into Naples.

Antonio   No he didn't. He told me he'd sleep here. After the fireworks it was too late to drive back.

Fabio   That was before the accident.

Antonio   What accident?

Fabio   Have your breakfast, Don Anto'. Then I'll tell you.

Antonio   Serious?

Fabio   Serious, no – otherwise they'd have woken you – but unfortunate, yes. Very unfortunate. I wasn't here, Sadly. Or I . . .

Antonio   Where's Armida? Where is she?

Immacolata *enters carrying an oval 19th-century tray, decorated with painted flowers, on which are a jug of milk, two glasses, a huge round loaf of peasant bread and a razor-sharp bread knife. She puts the tray on the table.*

Immacolata   Here we are. I'll go and get the ham and figs.

Antonio   Stay where you are. Tell me.

Fabio   You tell him, Immacolata. You were here.

Immacolata   Tell him what?

Antonio (*turns to look at her: icily*)   Perhaps you'd be good enough to inform me – what has happened to my wife?

Immacolata   Donna Armida suffered a dog bite.

Antonio (*thinks about it: no reaction*)   When?

He picks up the large round loaf and with the sharp knife begins to cut a slice towards his chest. Then, quite violently, he throws the knife onto the table in front of **Fabio** *and then he throws the loaf. This is not to make a point. It's how he always does it.*

Immacolata (*filling two glasses with milk*)   After midnight – nearer one. The rest of us had gone to bed.

Gives them each a glass of milk.

Donna Armida's always last up – getting things ready for morning. I heard a scream, and by the time I got to her she was more dead than alive – dress ripped – spattered with blood.

Antonio *is impassive – he listens to this account as if it were no business of his. He dips chunks of bread in his milk and sucks and mumbles it.* **Fabio** *eats and drinks with him.*

Gennaro and Amedeo drove her into casualty in Naples. I really wanted to call you but Donna Armida said, 'No, no. He never gets a decent night's sleep – let him rest.'

Antonio (*moved by the story but affecting coldness*)   Good fresh milk . . . Bread and milk in the morning . . . The only way to start the day.

Immacolata   The only way. That's what I always say.

Fabio   You should drink a glass at bedtime too.

Antonio   No I shouldn't. So where is she?

Immacolata   Still in town. At Amedeo's. He took her straight there once they let her out of hospital.

Antonio   Has Amedeo rung us yet?

Immacolata   About half-past two – to say his Mamma was still drowsy after the anaesthetic but as soon as she was feeling better he'd drive her out here.

Antonio   Who did it? Munaciello or Malavita?

Immacolata   I don't know. She never said.

Antonio   I shouldn't think it was Munaciello. Munaciello has a highly developed sense of fair play – also there's no doubting the affection he feels for Armida. Malavita – the gangster – he has no social graces at all. In fact he respects nobody.

Fabio   They're both bad dogs.

Sensing the possibility of an argument, **Immacolata** *moves away and gets on with her work.*

Antonio   Then there was this . . . other problem. Palummiello and Nait?

Fabio   Yes.

Antonio   What happened?

Fabio   They're out there.

Indicates the balcony.

You know what these people are. They tried to shoot each other – and for no good reason as far as I can see. I shouldn't think you'd want to get involved.

Antonio   So who said they could wait?

Fabio   They asked to see their Councillor. A consultation. I . . . I imagine they want you to arbitrate.

Immacolata *returns pushing in a portable clothes rack on which is* **Antonio***'s suit, shirt, tie, handkerchief, shoes, socks and a jewel box containing a watch, cufflinks, heavy gold rings, etc. She helps him off with his dressing gown, etc.*

Antonio   Now. Tell me, Doctor: have you made up your mind yet?

Fabio   Don Anto' – I think you know me well enough: sincere in thought, word and deed –

Antonio   The question was: 'Have you made up your mind?'

Fabio   Don Anto' – let's not be foolish about this: I know the thought of my leaving is distressing you. After a partnership of thirty-five years – and if you'll permit me to say so – thirty-five years of friendship – I can see the decision I've made must be upsetting – and yes, it makes the task you've set yourself – sworn to see through to the end – a task on which we have always worked together as one – very much more difficult. At the risk of sounding presumptuous I'll go so far as to say I have been your right arm. I've supported you for almost three-quarters of your life . . . Can we agree on this much?

Antonio (*appears to be taking little notice of* **Fabio**. **Immacolata** *has helped him put on his trousers, socks, shoes and shirt. He watches as she takes his gold cufflinks out of their box.*)   'Macula, I've told you – Cufflinks are not your job. Please examine your hands. Sweat and kitchen grease?

Immacolata (*showing them*)   Can you see any dirt?

Antonio (*curt*)   Call Geraldina.

Immacolata   As you wish. I'll call Geraldina.

Exit.

Antonio   'Can we agree on this much?' Get on with it.

Fabio (*with feeling*)   I'm tired of going over and over the same old, barren ground.

Antonio   So when are you off?

Fabio   Day after tomorrow. I already have my air-ticket.

Antonio (*concealing his true feelings*)   Friday then . . . You're sure you want to fly on a Friday? Friday the thirteenth . . . (*sighs*) It's up to you of course . . . However you travel, whichever plane you take . . . Sooner or later I suppose you'll end up in . . . New York.

Fabio (*worried*)   So what are you saying? Have I your blessing?

Antonio   I'll arrange for some friends to meet you at the airport: a reception committee.

Fabio   Don Anto', that's a threat.

Antonio   A piece of advice, you would say.

His sincerity is born of the fact that he believes what he is saying – that his judgments are absolute, fearless and without favour.

Each night as soon as my head touches the pillow I'm asleep. How is this possible? Only because my conscience is clear. It's always clear. When I make up my mind about a thing – decide a person's fate – and in this case it's your own fate we're discussing – before I pronounce final judgment I must convince myself that there is no possible alternative. Then I must advise the person concerned – in this case you – what the natural consequences – the outcome – of a certain course of action must be. You're with me?

Geraldina *enters followed by* **Immacolata**.

Geraldina   Papa! Good morning. (*Embraces him lovingly.*)

Antonio   Dina – Papa's little girl – help me with my shirt.

Geraldina   Don't I get a kiss first?

She kisses him on both cheeks – right and then left.

Did you sleep well?

Antonio   No. Only a little.

Geraldina (*holding out her hands*)   Inspection. Clean hands. I'll do your cufflinks.

Antonio   Where's Gennaro?

Immacolata   Choosing a tie for you. He asked me which suit you were wearing, and when I showed him the tie I'd picked out (*showing him it*) he said it would clash.

Antonio (*pleased*)   He'll bring me four or five to choose from but, whatever I say, I'll end up wearing the one he likes best. You'll see. Oho!

Gennaro *enters.*

Gennaro   Good morning, Papa.

He is carrying half a dozen ties – each a very different design – which would all go well with the suit **Antonio** *is wearing.*

Antonio   Good morning, my boy. Do I get a kiss?

They kiss.

Gennaro (*showing the ties*)   See which you like best.

Immacolata (*showing the one she had chosen*)   This is a nice one. What's wrong with this one?

Gennaro   A man's tie is part of his personality. Taste is a matter for his own judgment. Papa has never needed advisors.

(*To* **Antonio**.) So choose.

Antonio   Which do you like best?

Gennaro   This one.

A bold, colourful silk.

Antonio   Gennari', am I, or am I not, seventy-five years old? Will you ever get that into your head? What sort of an impression would I make – a tie like this!

Gennaro   Seventy-five? I don't see an old man.

Antonio   See what you like. I feel old.

Geraldina   No, Papa, you're still a *young* man. Young.

She hugs and kisses him.

Gennaro   Just make up your mind that this tie goes best with this suit and you'll find nobody will disagree with you.

Antonio   All right, all right. Give it here. Anything for a quiet life.

He takes the tie his son has chosen and starts to put it on.

What time are you going?

Gennaro   If you want a lift you'll have to hurry.

Antonio   No, I'm working from here today.

Gennaro   I have to go into town. Three big design jobs – for three pairs of newlyweds – Signed the contracts – agreed a price – taken the deposits. Guess how much I stand to make?

Antonio   No. It's none of my business.

Gennaro   I think you'd be pleased.

Antonio   I'm pleased if you are pleased.

(*To* **Immacolata**.) Have you fed the dogs?

Immacolata   Not yet.

Geraldina   You've heard what happened to Mamma?

Gennaro   Papa, if you'll allow me, I'll put down the one that did it.

Geraldina   Poor creature!

Immacolata   Poor creature! What about your poor mother? It half killed her.

Gennaro   A bullet between the eyes is sometimes the only solution.

Immacolata   Sad though. I was getting quite attached to Malavita. Still, for all our sakes, he's better off dead. Don Anto' I haven't fed them as I wasn't sure if you'd want me to put out two bowls of meat or just the one.

Antonio (*to his son*)   They're my dogs. It's my business. Keep your nose out of my affairs. And you – (*To* **Immacolata**.) Feed both of them . . . same as always.

Immacolata   Well, it's up to you.

Antonio *is now dressed;* **Geraldina** *hands him his watch and chain and his rings, including a heavy gold one; she studies him with admiration.*

Oh, how handsome you are, Papa!

She hugs and kisses him.

People keep saying to me 'But when are you going to get married?' and I ask them: where could I ever find a man like my Papa?

She takes his slippers, dressing gown, etc. back to his room; **Immacolata** *clears the table;* **Gennaro** *takes away the rejected ties.*

Fabio (*nervously*)   Don Anto', you were explaining to me . . .

Antonio   Yes. About your leaving.

Fabio   About my leaving.

Antonio   Doctor, Our Lord has allotted you a certain number of years . . . within the limits He has fixed, you are master of your own life: you can live out your full span of years or you can cut them short – it could be over in a matter of minutes. And if you chose to leave me you have my word – the word of Don Antonio Barracano – it's minutes.

Fabio *goes pale.*

Antonio   So is this what you'd call a threat? You know how things are with me . . . How could you possibly think such a thing? (*Hurt.*) A threat? I threaten nobody, we both know that. One man threatens another in the hopes of getting something out of him. Yes? And if he fails to get whatever it is he wants, it becomes pointless to carry out the threat, so everything goes back to how it was in the first place . . . And the man who made the threat – well, he's seen for what he is: just so much hot air. No. What I have done is to come to a judgment. So now – with the facts in front of you – you can make your decision. You do see why it's not a threat? Simply – you've just been given a free consultation.

Fabio   And in thirty-five years have you never had cause to doubt the soundness of your judgment? Have you never wished you could call back the sentences you pass on people?

Antonio (*thinks about it*)   Yes, I have.

Fabio (*looks sheepish, then decides on plain speaking*)   And I, Don Anto' – I have come to understand the truth of things – at last! – the truth of what I am. I'm your dupe – a great baby – and you are completely and utterly insane.

Antonio   D'you really think so?

Calmly, as if considering it possible.

It is possible I suppose.

Fabio (*exasperated by his calmness*)   You're a dreamer. Believe me, you are! I'm your doctor! It's your doctor telling you this! You're mad! Mad! Barking mad! All these years I've been fooling myself – I believed in you – I believed in the task we set ourselves – in justice – our noble project! But I've grown old, and feeble-minded – thirty years! And now I see the truth – a lifetime . . . wasted in the service of a rabble of petty thieves and gangsters – a disgrace to the mothers that bore them! You and I – we've risked jail not once or twice – thousands of times, and for so much riff-raff – the lowest dregs of society –

Antonio   The lowliest – I think you meant to say 'lowliest'. Yes, victims. Outcasts.

Fabio   Victims?

Antonio   Because nobody teaches them the rules of the game. Society grows fat on the ignorance of these people. The crimes and misdemeanours they commit just keep the

infernal machinery turning. And the ignorant understand.
They understand: 'Blessed are the pure in heart for they
shall see God.' But then they say: 'If we go to the courts to
settle our disputes, even with all the right in the world on
our side, perhaps our accusers – pure in heart and on their
way to see God though they are – might just have taken it
into their heads to perjure themselves, or bribe the jury!' It
does happen. What did our Lord Jesus Christ tell us? 'Thou
shalt not bear false witness!' He certainly knew the system.
I tell you, Doctor, even in His day they were all at it. And
nothing has changed!

Imitating the voice of a judge.

'Do you swear to tell the truth, the whole truth and nothing
but the truth?' And the perjurers swear their worthless
oaths. 'So expose their perjuries,' you'll say to me. But
what's the good? There's no proof, there's no evidence,
and anyway the jury's been bought and sold and so has the
judge. Not only does our good man lose his case, he gets
costs awarded against him. And then the perjurers sue him
for defamation of character! Character! So an ignorant man
must abandon all hope of the courts – courts are places
of great danger to him. He must take justice into his own
hands – settle his own case. It's true he may end up in prison
– so what? – his opponent ends up in the cemetery . . .
Doctor, have I not been such an executioner? Giacchino the
watchman: do you know why I killed him?

Fabio   No. I've never wanted to know.

Antonio   Oh believe me, I had good reason. Ten thousand
good reasons. The little liar had to die. I gave the court a
perfect alibi backed up by eight false witnesses. They said it
was self-defence. To this day I have no criminal record. I've
even kept my firearms licence.

Fabio   And the moral of the story?

Antonio   'Blessed are the pure in heart, for they shall see
God', while the ones who are in danger of being caught
out . . .

Fabio   Can go to Hell?

Antonio   No. They can come to me.

Fabio   Yes. Where you offer them a kind of rough justice –
try to keep the peace . . . But Don Anto' these are people for
whom killing each other is like running over a rabbit in the
road.

Antonio   But think of the crime – the violence we've
prevented! In thirty-five years? – It adds up.

Fabio   It adds up to a drop in the ocean. This task you've
set yourself – it's out of all proportion – it's futile! And
now I'm worn out – sick of piecing together smashed
skulls, stitching stomachs, fishing bullets out of legs, arms,
shoulders . . .

*He begins to lose control of his body and his speech; his right arm
begins to tremble; the pitch of his voice reflects a mounting hysteria.*

It was an unlucky day – the day I met you – and I've paid
the price – Thirty-five years your prisoner! A hostage! Three
times – Three times my brother's paid for my ticket to New
York – I want to be with him – end my life in peace – regain
some dignity – and this is the third time you've denied me
that opportunity. Why wait? Don't have me killed in New
York – Kill me here!

Opens his arms and thrusts out his chest.

Come on! Get on with it!

Shouts out at the top of his voice.

I was an honourable man! In an honourable profession! –
Oreste Della Ragione, my father, was Professor of Medicine
at the University of Naples for forty years! Forty years!

Stamps and weeps like a baby.

I've dishonoured his name – I'm rotten through and
through – I've buggered my life!

Falls down, with comic effect in a convenient armchair.

I've buggered everything! There's nothing left of me! Oh bugger, bugger!

Geraldina (*who has come in at the end of this*)   Is something the matter with him?

Immacolata *comes in, worried.*

Gennaro (*entering*)   Dina? What is it?

Fabio (*for the rest of his scene shaking so much he finds it difficult to get the words out*)   I have to lie down.

Taking his own pulse.

Feverish. In five minutes I'll be flat out.

Immacolata (*concerned*)   Poor Doctor –

Gennaro   I'll get him a glass of cognac –

Fabio   Just get me to bed.

Shaking and gibbering.

What about a hot-water bottle, 'Macula?

Immacolata *goes;* **Geraldina** *and* **Gennaro** *start to help him to his room.*

Fabio   Yes. Put me to bed, please. What about a water bottle – what about a . . . what . . . what about . . .

Antonio (*who has seemed oblivious to the Doctor's distress, now strikes home*)   Better put off the trip to New York? If you're ill? Don't you think so, my friend?

Fabio   You may be right . . .

Antonio   And when you're well again . . . What do you think you'll do? Leave us?

Fabio (*after a moment's thought*)   Who knows? When I'm well again . . . When I'm well again . . .

The three go out. **Catiello** *comes in through the French windows.*

Catiello   Don Anto', may I . . .

Antonio   Who've we got?

Pleased with himself.

Catiello   Pascale Nasone and Vicienzo Cuozzo are waiting. And Rafiluccio Santaniello with his girlfriend.

Antonio   Who's Rafiluccio Santaniello?

Catiello   From the pastry shop.

Antonio   Ah. Anybody else?

Enter **Geraldina**.

Catiello   Nait and Palummiello – out there – They're respectfully begging a consultation.

Antonio   Dina.

Geraldina   Papa?

Antonio   Look in the desk. Get me the file on Cuozzo and Nasone.

Geraldina (*looking through the files*)   Nasone, Nasone, Nasone . . . Cuozzo, Cuozzo, Cuozzo . . . Where is it?

Antonio (*to* **Catiello**)   Show them in.

Catiello   All of them at once?

Antonio   All of them at once.

Catiello   Right.

Exit.

Geraldina   Here.

Putting the file in front of him.

Antonio   Who's claiming what?

Geraldina   Pascale Nasone is claiming repayment of three hundred thousand lire he lent Vicienzo Cuozzo.

Antonio   Ah, yes, with interest at ten per cent the first week, and after that forty per cent per month. Three hundred thousand.

Geraldina   Right.

Antonio   And Santaniello?

Geraldina   We've nothing on file. He's very young. Perhaps this is his first appointment?

Antonio   Nait and Palummiello?

Geraldina   They're the two involved in this morning's shooting.

Antonio   Ah. The ones that woke me up.

Catiello *ushers in* **Vicienzo**, **Nasone**, **Rafiluccio**, **Rita**, **Nait** *and* **Palummiello**.

Catiello   In you go.

Vicienzo (*hat in hand, bows respectfully*)   Don Antonio.

Nasone   At your service, Don Anto'.

Antonio *doesn't seem to notice them.*

Rafiluccio (*bows*)   Good morning, Don Antonio.

Antonio   Good morning. You're Arturo Santaniello's son?

Rafiluccio   Yes, sir. And this is my fiancée.

Antonio (*after a pause in which he studies* **Rita**, *who is very pregnant, chokes back an astonished laugh, and mutters something to himself*)   Ah! I see the baby's invited to the wedding.

Rafiluccio (*happy*)   We hope so.

Antonio   What can I do for you?

Rafiluccio   Don Antonio, it's complicated. To tell you the truth – to speak plainly – man to man –

Antonio   Stop there. I suspect this is going to take some time.

Indicating the balcony.

Be good enough to take your fiancée outside for a while – she looks as if she needs some air. I'll deal with these few small matters and then I'll call you.

Rafiluccio   Of course, Don Antonio.

(*To* **Rita**.) Let me –

He helps her onto the balcony.

Antonio   Nait? Palummiello?

Nait   Don Antonio.

Bows.

Palummiello   Sir.

Bows.

Don Antonio.

Antonio   Sit over there.

Nait   Thank you, sir.

Helps **Palummiello** *to a chair upstage.*

Antonio (*to* **Nasone**)   How's life?

Nasone   Oh, nothing changes, Don Anto'. My sister's had another baby – number six this one – two boys and four girls.

Antonio   Ah. Heaven has blessed you.

Nasone   Yes, it certainly has, praise God, praise God. We mustn't complain.

Antonio   And we must settle our differences.

Nasone   What differences?

Antonio   Vicienzo has children too.

Vicienzo   Six.

Nasone   Yes, Heaven has blessed even Vicienzo Cuozzo.
Surprising really.

Antonio   Pasca', let's come to the point – time is pressing
– I was in town the other day – settling a few debts – and I
bumped into our friend here (*indicating* **Vicienzo**). 'Vicienzo,
good to see you!' 'Don Antonio long time no see' – you know
how it is. I knew his father – a real gentleman – my friend.
My friend . . . 'So how are you doing, Vicienzo?' Well, it
turns out his family's staring destitution in the face . . . and
because of you . . . For a loan of three hundred thousand
on which he's been paying thirty thousand a week for seven
months! . . . So now, Pascale, he's going to shoot you.

Nasone   Shoot me!

Vicienzo (*shaking with desperation*)   He's ruined me, Don
Anto' . . . me and my children. A hundred and twenty
thousand a month I've been paying him and that's just the
interest – for seven months! . . . And he's still demanding
repayment of the original three hundred thousand. My
children are starving to death! He's a bloodsucker – he
doesn't know what pity is. Every month it gets worse. My
wife's had to sell the bed we slept on – my brand new Sunday
suit – that's had to go too –

Nasone   But why? When you wanted the money you
seemed happy with my terms. Don't say you didn't know
it would have to be repaid. If you'd paid it back within the
week you'd have had a very good deal – three hundred
thousand for a mere thirty. Don Anto', is it my fault that
some people have no head for business?

Vicienzo   Business! I borrowed the money because my
child had to have an operation –

Nasone   So you say, but if you don't pay what you owe me
then I'm the one who suffers . . . I have a family too.

Vicienzo   Yes, God knows you have, and a flashy new car,
and rooms you rent to your tarts, and a wife who screws her
pick-ups in your own bedroom, while you sit downstairs
counting the money –

Nasone   Look, I'd be happy to discuss family values with you – all day if necessary – but first pay back the money I lent you. I want my money!

Antonio (*looking at his watch*)   May we bring this meeting to a close?

Nasone   What sort of a close? You say he's going to shoot me? Well if he's planning to spend the next thirty years in jail –

Antonio   No, Pascale. You've misunderstood. He *was* going to kill you . . . but then, last night, he came to me –

Vicienzo (*who did no such thing; puzzled*)   Don Anto' . . . Last night –

Antonio (*coldly*)   Shut up. Yes, last night, when you came here and handed over the three hundred thousand –

Vicienzo   I –

Antonio   Stop interrupting – Vicienzo has given me your three hundred thousand. For safekeeping.

Nasone   Why didn't he give it directly to me?

Antonio   Because he can't pay last month's interest on the original loan. So he's asked me to speak for him. And I'm asking you to write off the final payment – do the decent thing. Think about it. In seven months your three hundred thousand has brought you in a profit of eight hundred and forty thousand. So my advice to you . . . is to be satisfied with what you've got. Let it end here.

Nasone   Ha!

Delighted at the prospect of getting his capital back.

How could I refuse any request of Don Antonio Barracano? His smallest wish is, to me, a command!

Antonio   Have you brought the papers?

Nasone (*taking the IOU out of his wallet*)   Here we are!

Antonio (*delicately taking it as if it's something rather dirty*)   Allow me?

Nasone   Of course.

Antonio   It's all in ten thousand lire notes.

Nasone   Oh, never mind. I have deep pockets!

Antonio   I know you do. Dina, just look in the drawer, would you?

Geraldina   Which drawer, Papa?

Looks at the table which has no drawer.

Antonio   This drawer.

Opening an imaginary drawer in the table.

Here we have . . . In each of these three envelopes there's a hundred thousand lire.

Takes imaginary rubber bands off the imaginary envelopes and throws them one by one on the table.

One. Two. Three. I've counted it and it's all there, but I'd like you to check it . . . Better do it here. Now.

Nasone (*who doesn't get what's happening*)   Do what, Don Anto'?

Antonio   Count it.

Nasone   Count what, Don Anto'?

Antonio   The money – the three hundred thousand I'm giving you.

Nasone   But . . . Don Anto' . . . ?

Antonio (*icily; fixing* **Nasone** *with a steely gaze*)   Count it.

Fascinated and terrified, **Nasone** *begins to count the imaginary notes.* **Antonio** *joins in from time to time. The other are impressed and amused.*

Nasone   One, two, three, four, five, six, seven, eight, nine, ten –

Antonio   – And one hundred. Keep counting.

Nasone   One, two, three, four, five, six, seven, eight, nine, ten.

Antonio   That's two hundred. Now the third.

Handing him the final envelope.

Nasone   One, two, three, four, five, six, seven, eight, nine, ten.

Antonio   Good. Happy now?

Nasone   Yes, sir.

Antonio   Shake hands. And no more nonsense between you.

Vicienzo   Willingly.

Puts out his hand.

Nasone   Anything you say.

Antonio   Good. Everybody's happy.

Nasone   So . . . I'd better go.

Moves towards the door.

Antonio   Hey! Haven't you forgotten something? Take your money.

Nasone (*who has had enough of the joke*)   Oh, Don Anto' . . .

Antonio (*icy*)   Take it.

Nasone *returns to the table, puts the imaginary money in his inside jacket pocket and leaves full of wounded pride.*

Antonio (*to* **Vicienzo**, *picking up the IOU*)   Is this what he made you sign?

Vicienzo   Yes, sir.

Antonio   Well then . . .

Tears it up.

Vicienzo (*overcome with joy and tears he can hardly speak*)   Don Anto', may you live to be a hundred. Don Anto' you've saved my life – my family – my children –

Seizes his hands and kisses them.

These are the hands of a saint –

Tries to kiss his feet.

Antonio   No – Vicienzo – get up. I'm not a saint . . .

Geraldina *and* **Catiello** *help* **Vicienzo** *to his feet, and help him out of the room.*

Vicienzo (*in tears*)   You're a father to us, Don Anto' – you're a father to every poor man in Naples – we pray to you – we pray for you – all of us – we'd give our lives for you, Don Anto' –

Catiello   That's enough now. Don Antonio knows how grateful you are – come on –

Geraldina   Papa has other people to see . . .

Vicienzo (*just before he's hurried away*)   He's our Papa too! Everybody's Papa!

He's heard shouting similar things a few times as he goes out, then off down the street.

Antonio   We must press on. Who's next?

Geraldina (*looking at the list*)   Santaniello.

Nait   There's us as well.

Antonio   What are you?

Nait   Nait.

Antonio (*looking at* **Palummiello** *who comes up to him*)   He shot you in the leg?

Palummiello   Yes, sir. I'm Palummiello.

Antonio *invites* **Nait** *to begin*.

Nait   The port's my territory. When the American sailors
come ashore I team up with them and when I find one
who's queer I take him to the Colorado to be fleeced – it's
a nightclub on the via Marina. Now, I've not been too well
lately – night life doesn't really suit me – it's so hot and
damp in those clubs – I've been in bed for three weeks with
bronchitis and pneumonia. So this arsehole goes to the
people who run the Colorado and persuades them to let him
take over my job. Don Anto' he's stolen the bread from my
mouth.

Palummiello   I never went to them. They came to me.

Antonio (*to* **Palummiello**) What part of town are you from?

Palummiello   Montecalvario.

Antonio   And you?

Nait   Sanità.

Antonio   Ah! That's my district. Do you have a gun?

Nait   Yes, sir – Don Anto'.

Antonio   Put it on the table.

He does.

Law and order has broken down. On two counts. First: the
offence committed by Palummiello against Nait.

(*To* **Palummiello**.) The Colorado Club's in his district. So you
keep out of it. You're taking the bread from his mouth. Do
we understand each other?

Palummiello   Yes, sir.

Antonio   We'll be watching you.

Palummiello   It won't be necessary.

Antonio   Second: the offence committed by Nait . . . against
me.

Nait (*worried*)   Don Anto'? –

Antonio   Palummiello was in the wrong – certainly he was – but, tell me, do you have the right to decide his punishment? A bullet in the leg? You belong to my district? Sanità? So why didn't you come and consult me before you decided to shoot him? What were you afraid of?

Nait   Don Anto' – he started it and if he wants another –

Antonio   Is there no end to it? Have you no respect for a man's life? I shoot you, you shoot me . . . then everybody joins in: brothers, fathers, uncles, the in-laws – it's a massacre, it's war! It stops here or I'll see you're thrown into jail – you're in Sanità – my district – and I'll see you starve there, you'll die of thirst – you'll live like the lice in your filthy shirts. This incident is over. Shake hands.

They look at each other for a moment, then shake hands with relief and affection; **Antonio** *takes a heavy gold ring from his right hand and places it in his left.*

And remember this . . .

Nait   Me, sir?

Antonio (*suddenly cracks* **Nait** *across the face with a strength surprising for an old man;* **Nait** *is stunned by the blow*)   The next time you want to take the law into your own hands – the next time you want to blow somebody's brains out – don't ask Don Antonio Barracano to sweep up the mess you make. You want to shoot somebody, you ask me first. First! Understood?

Picks up the gun and hands it to him.

Take your gun and get out.

Stunned, **Nait** *takes the gun.* **Palummiello** *sees* **Nait** *is unsteady and, though hobbling himself, helps him towards the door. The others watch, tense.*

Palummiello (*after a pause*)   Shall we go?

Pushes him on. **Nait** *moves towards the door as if in a dream.*
Antonio *ignores what is happening. At the door* **Nait** *turns and*
stares at **Antonio**. **Palummiello** *watches, worried.* **Nait** *slowly*
lifts his right arm; we think he might be going to shoot **Antonio** *then*
he turns the weapon towards himself and studies it. He puts it in his
pocket.

Nait (*with an apologetic smile*)   Goodbye for now.

Antonio   Call Santaniello.

Rafiluccio *and* **Rita** *come in off the balcony.*

Rafiluccio   I'm here, Don Anto'.

Antonio   So sit down and let's hear what you have to tell us.
It's complicated you say?

Rafiluccio   Thank you.

Pulls up a chair for **Rita** *and sits next to her.*

Antonio   So?

Rafiluccio   You don't remember me?

Geraldina   I do. Your father has the cake shop in via
Giacinto Albino.

Rafiluccio   He has two shops now.

Geraldina   Really? He's doing well then.

Rafiluccio   The old place in Giacinto Albino's the same as
it always was but he's had another in via Roma for the last
couple of years – more up-market – double-fronted – a little
gold mine. All the smart set get their bread there.

Geraldina   My school was in Giacinto Albino. Every
morning I used to buy a ham roll at your place. I'll bet you
don't remember me.

Rafiluccio   I do.

Geraldina   There was that lady who used to serve behind the counter – the nice-looking one – dark hair – always wore a pretty gold necklace –

Rafiluccio   My mother. I lost her when I was only six. During the war our part of town took quite a pounding . . . She had heart trouble – she couldn't bear to be crowded into the bomb-shelters – we lived on the first floor. One night the flats opposite us took a direct hit – three big bombs . . . Fate, I suppose . . . A piece of shrapnel flew through the window and struck my mother here (*points to his throat*). Three minutes later she was in a better world.

Geraldina   Poor thing!

Antonio   Do you think we could come to the point?

Rafiluccio   Don Anto', I'd prefer to discuss this man to man; it's a very delicate matter –

Immacolata *enters in haste.*

Immacolata   It's your mother! She's home – Donna Armida –

Geraldina (*rushing out to meet her*)   Mamma! Mamma's back –

Donna Armida *arrives supported by* **Amedeo**, *her son.* **Gennaro** *follows them in.* **Armida** *is still attractive, about forty-five, pale, tired. She has a cardigan around her shoulders; her hair is fixed with tortoiseshell combs; she is heavily bandaged about her left side and breast. She is moved by her daughter's greeting.*

Armida   Darling child!

Geraldina *wants to embrace her but* **Armida** *flinches;* **Geraldina** *sees what's wrong and stops herself.*

Armida   No! No . . . be careful – It feels as if it's on fire.

Pointing to her breast; she sees her husband.

Oh Anto'!

Antonio   My darling Armi' . . . What have you been doing to yourself?

Immacolata   You're so pale.

Amedeo   Twelve stitches.

Mother and son go to **Antonio**.

Armida   Anto', look what he did to me!

Fighting back tears but smiling for her husband's sake.

Amedeo   It was Malavita.

Gennaro   Papa, just say the word – Let me deal with Malavita.

Takes out his gun.

Amedeo   Look, don't take offence – but I've promised myself – I'll take care of Malavita.

Takes out his gun.

Armida (*motherly concern*)   Be careful with those guns, boys. Somebody may get hurt –

Antonio   Not so fast! Armi', darling, there's something you must tell me – and you two – if Malavita has to die then we'll need only one gun and that gun will be mine . . . Armi', when Malavita savaged you where did it happen? Did he come into your room?

Armida   No.

Antonio   And what time was it?

Armida   One in the morning . . . I was in the chicken-run . . . collecting eggs . . . for breakfast.

Antonio   In the chicken-run, eh? Armi', darling, how much would you say I loved you.

Armida   Very much.

Antonio   And how much do you love me?

Armida   Anto' . . .

Surprised he feels the need to ask.

Antonio   Last night you were in pain, but now, at this moment, who would you say is feeling the most pain? Me or you?

Armida (*believing it*)   You.

Antonio   You will carry a scar on your left breast. Where will I carry my scar?

Armida (*moved*)   On your heart.

Antonio   Malavita is our guard dog. Our watchman. He protects our house, our family . . . And our chickens. Armi', darling, you provoked Malavita.

(*To his sons.*) Put away your guns.

They do.

The dog was perfectly justified in attacking you. Don't you see?

No one protests; **Armida** *seems happy with the verdict.*

Antonio   Now . . . how are you feeling?

Armida (*disguising the pain she feels*)   Better. I think I'll go and lie down.

Immacolata   Yes, you must. Come on, then. Then I'll fetch you a nice bowl of soup.

Immacolata *and the children help her to her room.*

Armida   They said I'll have to have an anti-rabies jab.

Amedeo   There's no need. I'll go and get the vet to certify the dogs are OK. The health authorities will want to examine Malavita too.

Rafiluccio   Don Anto' . . .

Antonio   My boy, I'm sorry, but you see how things are today. Why don't you come back tomorrow?

Rafiluccio   Don Anto', it won't wait. It's gone too far for that.

Antonio   Twenty-four hours – it's not the end of the world.

Going to the door.

Rafiluccio   Don Anto', tomorrow morning I'm going to kill my father.

Antonio (*stops at the door, turns and stares at the boy in disbelief;* **Rita** *bursts into tears then tries to stifle her sobs; the two men don't seem to notice her; pause*)   What are you saying?

Rafiluccio (*calm*)   Tomorrow morning I'm going to kill my father.

Antonio (*takes in the seriousness of the case and pities them; he looks at them for a while*)   You've thought it through? You're convinced there's no possible alternative?

Rafiluccio (*calmly*)   I have. I am.

Antonio   So. We must certainly give the matter some thought – a great deal of thought. Can you come back in two hours?

Rafiluccio   In two hours? Yes, Don Antonio.

He bows.

He puts his arm on **Rita**'s *shoulder, prompting her to stand up. As they leave she is trying to fight back her sobs and tears. They go out into the grounds of the house.* **Antonio** *watches them for a while, listening. Then he goes slowly, head bowed, to his wife's room.*

Act Two

The same room almost two hours later. **Armida**, **Fabio**, **Geraldina** *and* **Immacolata** *waiting*.

Armida   What time is it?

Fabio (*glances at his watch*)   Quarter to nine.

Armida   What can have happened to Anto'? Why isn't he back?

Geraldina   He's taken Malavita to be examined for rabies . . . by the health authorities. I expect he's been held up.

Immacolata   They'll be ages yet. They've been gone less than an hour.

Armida   Why didn't Gennaro go with them?

Geraldina   You know he can't bear to be away from his beloved shop –

Armida   Where's Amedeo?

Immacolata   Don Antonio sent him back into Naples on some urgent business – all very mysterious – I couldn't make out what it was about, but I heard Don Antonio say: 'Just trust me, Amedeo; put him in the car and bring him here as fast as you can.'

Armida   Bring who?

Immacolata   I haven't a clue.

Armida (*to* **Fabio**)   Then you should be with him. He's on his own. You know how I worry when he has nobody to –

Fabio   My dear lady, I'm just getting over an attack of nerves – Look! I'm still trembling – It's true! – ask Immacolata.

Immacolata   I suppose it must be. He had two hot-water bottles.

Fabio   I should still be in bed.

Geraldina   Whenever you make up your mind to leave us you start shaking.

Fabio   Perhaps I'm allergic to America. Perhaps its unhealthy influence reaches right across the Atlantic – across the Mediterranean – into the Bay of Naples and –

Armida (*still worrying about* **Antonio**)   How far away are these health-authority kennels?

Fabio   This isn't the first time Don Antonio's dogs have been put into quarantine. Stop worrying.

Armida   If he thinks his dogs are being treated unfairly he may fly off the handle – and when all's said and done the authorities are the authorities – they have the power. But as far as Anto's concerned that will just provoke him even more.

Fabio   You think so? Well, he's your husband . . . but Don Antonio Barracano – nobody knows him as I do. You have never studied his behaviour in court where he bows and scrapes before the bench –

Armida (*defending her husband*)   Everybody behaves like that in front of the magistrates –

Fabio   No, no – it's the ushers too – everybody – the lowliest court official – anybody connected with the legal profession. Don Antonio knows better than anyone how to manipulate these people – how to get things done. I shouldn't be surprised if he persuades them to let him bring the dog home with him.

Armida   Let's hope not. Just at the moment I'm not feeling up to –

Geraldina   Last time Malavita savaged somebody that badly they kept him in quarantine for a couple of weeks.

Rafiluccio *rushes in, out of breath, and speaks to the women.*

Rafiluccio   Forgive me –

Armida (*alarmed*)   What's happened?

Immacolata   This young man's been waiting for some time; he's been talking to Don Antonio.

Geraldina   It's Rafiluccio Santaniello, Mamma.

Rafiluccio   Your servant, Donna Armida.

She is charmed by him.

Geraldina   What is it?

Rafiluccio   The young lady who came with me –

Immacolata   Isn't she still with you?

Rafiluccio   Yes. Don Antonio said we should come back in two hours – there's twenty minutes to go – But we were out there – over by the barn – we didn't know where else to go and – it must have been the sun – Rita's so delicate, you see – and now she's feeling ill and I don't know what to do –

Immacolata   Ah! Poor thing!

Geraldina   Where is she?

Rafiluccio   In the orchard – over there – to the right –

Immacolata (*prompting*)   Doctor . . .?

Fabio   I'm not going out in the sun – I'm ill too, you know! Bring her in here.

Geraldina   Come on, 'Macula.

They go towards the garden.

Immacolata   Come with us, boy.

He follows them out.

Fabio   I think he's the baker's son, from via Giacinto Albino.

Armida   Who's the girl?

Fabio   No idea. How are you feeling now, Donna Armi'?

Armida   A little better. Thanks.

Fabio   I was sorry not to have been here last night . . . when it happened. I'll send somebody to the chemist's to fetch you some painkillers. You may need something to help you sleep.

Armida   Thank you, Doctor.

Immacolata (*off*)   It's not much further.

Geraldina (*off*)   Gently does it. Let me help.

Rita (*off*)   Thank you. I'll be fine now. I was just feeling a little light-headed.

Geraldina *and* **Immacolata** *come in, supporting* **Rita**.

Immacolata   It'll be something and nothing.

They sit her near the table; **Rafiluccio** *stands in the doorway.*

Immacolata   A touch of sun, like your young man said. A little rest, a little fresh air, and you'll soon feel better.

Armida   She's not well at all – shouldn't you take a look at her, Doctor? I rather think the poor girl's expecting a baby.

This is a blinding insight into the very obvious.

Rafiluccio (*proudly*)   She is. In eight weeks.

Armida   She's your wife?

Rafiluccio (*proudly*)   She's my woman.

Immacolata   Come on, Doctor. Examine her.

Fabio   Why? What's the point? I too think she's pregnant. But that's not what's wrong with her – she's ill because she's starving.

(*Goes to* **Rita**.) Can't you see how pale she is? – the exhaustion in her eyes?

(*Takes one of her wrists.*) Let's see – no wonder – hardly any pulse. When did you last have a proper meal?

Rita *averts her eyes which fill with tears.*

Immacolata   What have you eaten today?

Rafiluccio (*stays where he is but answers bitterly for her*)   She's eaten nothing.

Fabio   Probably been in this state for months. The girl's suffering from malnutrition.

Rafiluccio   I don't doubt it.

Fabio   Oh? And what does that make you? Are you so proud of yourself? 'She's my woman!' So why don't you look after her?

Rafiluccio (*comes up to* **Fabio**)   Doctor, you've just examined her. Now look more closely. What do you see? She's nothing. Skin and bone. You'd not think twice about throwing her out with the rest of the rubbish. Don't you agree? Damaged goods – no use to anybody? Out she goes! She dresses well, don't you think? Hardly! Are those silk stockings she's wearing? No they're not. Has she just come from the hairdressers? I don't think she has. And yet this nothing – this being of skin and bone – such as it is – is mine – so pale – such eyes – look again – tell me she is nothing! She is my woman! And me – look at me – My suit –

Shows a tear.

What about – do you want to see the shirt?

Takes of his jacket; the shirt is full of holes and patches.

My sole is (*or if you wish to avoid the pun:* 'My shoes are') worn right through. Look.

Takes off his shoes; he has bare feet.

'What does that make me?' Isn't that what you asked? Am I proud of myself? No, I'm damaged goods too – no use to anybody – I'm just so much rubbish.

Kicks an imaginary bit of rubbish off an imaginary pavement.

But what am I to her? – That's what matters. I'm her man.

Rita (*enchanted*)   Oh, he's so beautiful!

Rafiluccio   I work at the docks – When there's anything going – there are always so many people looking for work – most of us get shut out. I'll do anything – labouring, portering, nightwatchman – anything I'm offered. Anything honourable. What money I earn I give to her. Half a loaf of bread for her and half for me when I'm working . . . half a loaf of nothing for her and half for me when I'm not.

Fabio   You could both starve to death you know?

Rafiluccio   Both? All three of us could starve to death. (*His hand on* **Rita**'s *baby*.) This is my son.

Fabio   Your sense of paternal responsibility is all very well, my boy – it does you credit – but if this girl doesn't eat something soon she'll pass out.

Armida (*concerned*)   'Macula . . .

Immacola (*doesn't need prompting; she hurries to the kitchen*)   I don't know! What sort of a world are we living in . . .

Fabio (*tears a sheet off the prescription pad he has been writing on and gives it to* **Rafiluccio**)   Go to the chemist's. Get them to make this up.

Rafiluccio   What, now?

Fabio   Yes, now. Your 'woman' will be perfectly safe with us.

Rafiluccio   Yes, but . . .

Rita (*trying to cover for him*)   He never carries money with him – he says he'd only lose it . . . So I look after it.

She produces a knotted handkerchief but she is too weak to undo the knot; she can't seem to focus; she tries twice and fails.

Rafiluccio   I'll do it. Let me try.

Undoes the knot; looks through the few things the handkerchief contains.

These are our bus tickets. If we lose them we'll be stuck here in Terzigno.

Puts them back.

Your bracelet.

A cheap one of reproduction coral.

Rita   It's broken. Don't lose the pieces.

Rafiluccio   Where's the money? Ah.

(*Looks at* **Fabio**.) Do you think three hundred lire will cover it?

Fabio   How should I know?

Armida   Tell them to charge it to Signora Barracano. We pay the account monthly.

Rafiluccio   How could I allow you to pay for our medicine?

Armida   It's nothing.

Rafiluccio   Forgive me, but we couldn't possibly accept.

Geraldina   But you must. Anyway, I owe you money.

Rafiluccio   What?

Geraldina   When I was at school and I used to come into your shop for my ham roll you always used to slip me a pastry when your father wasn't looking. I can't tell you how much I adored those pastries! If you calculate the cost of all my stolen cakes and then subtract the cost of the medicine you'll find that we're still in your debt.

Armida   Go on! You must hurry!

Rafiluccio (*moved*)   Forgive me . . .

Hurries out.

Immacolata *comes back with a big dish of thick soup, a loaf of bread, a plate of mozzarella, milk and fruit.*

Immacolata   The soup's very hot – and there's a chunk of meat in it.

Sets everything before **Rita**, *who does not eat.*

Armida   Miss . . . er . . . er . . . You must eat something.

Fabio   Try a little of the hot soup. A little soup first.

Geraldina   Yes, you must – there's soup, meat, a nice glass of milk . . . and this fresh mozzarella.

Rita *doesn't move.*

Armida   Won't you try to eat something?

Immacolata   Of course she will. She'll eat it when she's ready. Poor child, we're embarrassing her.

Geraldina   Would you prefer to be on your own?

Rita   I want Rafiluccio.

Geraldina   He's only gone to the chemist's. He'd want you to eat something.

Rita (*weakening*)   Perhaps . . .

Geraldina (*aside*)   We'd better leave her on her own. Or she won't touch it.

Immacolata   Yes, let's.

Armida   I won't be able to sleep tonight. There's a burning sensation all the way up my arm.

Immacolata   And you look absolutely dreadful. Pale . . . Ghastly.

Armida   Thank you so much.

Immacolata   Come on.

She and **Geraldina** *take* **Armida** *to her room.*

Fabio   I'll send Catiello for those painkillers.

He follows them out.

Rita, *after a brief pause, looks around, takes a fork and fishes out the meat from the soup; she looks disappointed that the piece of meat is so small. She sets it aside in a small bowl for* **Rafiluccio**, *which she covers to keep warm. At last she tastes the soup. She begins to eat hungrily.* **Antonio** *enters.*

Antonio (*watching her for a while – a smile on his face*)   Take your time. It's not a race.

Rita (*scared, lets the spoon drop, and starts from the table like a thief caught red handed*)   The lady of the house wanted me to eat it. I asked for nothing.

Antonio   And you must eat as much as you can. Come on. The soup's getting cold.

Rita   No – I've had enough, thank you. Though maybe I could try a little mozzarella.

Antonio   Of course. You must.

Cuts some cheese for **Rita** *and hands it to her.*

Rita   Thank you.

She starts to eat, self-consciously.

Antonio   You're young Rafiluccio's fiancée?

Rita   Not exactly his fiancée . . . no.

Antonio   It's what he told me.

Rita   It's how he introduces me. But in front of people he can trust he says: 'This is my woman.'

Antonio   And what do you understand by his use of: 'This is my woman.'

Rita   Oh, you must know.

Antonio   I know what it means to me. I want to know what it means to Rafiluccio Santaniello.

Rita   You say first. I'll finish this cheese then I'll tell you how he explains it.

Antonio   A man should never speak of his fiancée or his wife as 'my woman'. In both those cases I imagine the lady concerned would find the term offensive. A wife is a wife. 'This is my wife' is something a man should say with pride. A man who chooses his words carefully would say 'this is my woman' in only one of two cases. First, when it becomes necessary for a man to speak of his mistress – a kept woman we might say – and he wishes to show the people to whom he is speaking that he is an honourable, responsible and faithful sort of fellow. Second, in those unfortunate circumstances, when a man has hired a prostitute and some other man begins to proposition her, he would say: 'That's my woman! Get your hands off her!'

Rita   No – in your day, perhaps, it may have meant something like that, but your day . . . well it was some time ago, wasn't it? Today – no. To Rafiluccio it means something very different. Well . . . I never knew my parents. I was brought up by the Sisters of Mercy – at the orphanage della Misericordia in Torre del Greco. Eight years ago – when I was fifteen – I was working as a maid – for a good family who had taken me out of the orphanage and promised to look after me. And to tell you the truth they treated me well. I think of them with affection. The house was in a street which crossed Giacinto Albino. And in Giacinto Albino – for the whole time I was in service there – I used to go and buy our bread in Rafiluccio's father's shop. Do you think I could do that for seven years without noticing Rafiluccio or Rafiluccio noticing me? But all I ever said to him – every day for seven years – was: 'Two loaves of bread, please . . .' I'd take the bread from him, we'd say: 'Good morning', and that was all . . .

Antonio   But what's this got to do with –

Rita   You'll see. Be patient . . . One day – a year and a half ago – I was buying my bread when: 'Would you like to come with me to a film this evening?'

Antonio   At last! Rafiluccio spoke to you?

Rita   No. This was a young labourer who was buying some
pastries. 'I'm sorry,' I said, 'but I don't go to the cinema
with young men I don't know.' 'Oh, never mind,' he said,
'I'll take Rafiluccio instead – How about it Rafilu'?' 'No,'
said Rafiluccio, 'I can't make it this evening', and as he was
speaking he was looking straight into my eyes. 'Tonight at
nine, I've already arranged to meet someone in the foyer
of the cinema at Santa Lucia.' He never took his eyes from
mine. And I knew what he meant. So at nine o'clock, in the
foyer of the cinema at Santa Lucia, I first felt Rafiluccio's
arm slipping into mine. I thought I was dreaming. I never
spoke a word. I was waiting for him to speak first, and at last
he whispered, 'Are you in love with me?' And I said: 'I've
been in love with you for seven years! How long have I been
in your thoughts?' 'For seven years,' he said . . . The two of
us peopling a single thought. From that evening nothing
else has ever moved me – not people – nothing they say or
do is of interest to me; I don't notice shop windows, I don't
want to go to the cinema and if people talk to me I don't
listen to what they are saying. When I'm with Rafiluccio I
have everything – I'm at peace with myself – everything's
right. And Rafiluccio has explained to me that this is how
things are when one person is meant for another. It's like
this: a woman is only her true self – she only comes near her
true beauty – when she meets the one man who is made for
her. And the same is true for the man. I found Rafiluccio
and Rafiluccio found me. I am his woman. He is my man.

Antonio   Ah! Now that I can understand. An encounter
– two halves of the same soul. Tell me something. Has
Rafiluccio told you anything about the decision he has
made?

Rita   To shoot his father? (*Sadly nods her head.*) Yes.

(*Business with tears and a handkerchief.*) For the last three
months he's talked of nothing else. He's immovable. When
he says he'll do something he does it.

Antonio   But you think it's the wrong decision? Have you tried to reason with him?

Rita   Whenever we discuss it he manages to persuade me that there's no alternative. But when I'm on my own, and I start to think about what he says . . . But no . . . I don't think killing his father can be a good thing.

Antonio   How have you tried to make him change his mind?

Rafiluccio *appears and watches them from the French windows.*

Rita   How? What could I possibly say? For Rafiluccio – it's not something he's chosen to do – it's an obsession – it's chosen him. He can't sleep because of it . . . You must save him, Don Anto' – I know it will take a miracle . . . and only you can work it.

Rafiluccio   Forgive her, Don Anto' – the poor girl doesn't understand what she's asking nor of whom she's asking it. (*To* **Rita**.) I've told you, when I'm not with you, you must learn to keep your mouth shut.

Antonio   In fact she was only answering questions I put to her.

Rafiluccio   Her answer should have been: 'I don't know anything; ask Rafiluccio when he comes back.'

(**Rita** *looks tearful*.) And don't start crying again. That's enough! It's making you ill. All she ever does is cry . . .

Antonio   Well, my boy, if you've something to discuss with me, I'm at your service.

Rafiluccio   Rita, go outside – take a little walk while I speak to Don Antonio.

Rita   Let me stay here. Let me hear what Don Antonio has to say.

Rafiluccio (*unbending*)   No. Go for a walk – the fresh air will do you good.

Rita (*begging*)   Don Anto', I want to stay, tell him you want me to stay –

Enter **Geraldina**.

Geraldina   Papa, how did it go?

Antonio   They tell me there's nothing wrong with Malavita and we can have him back in a week . . . So that's OK.

Geraldina   And did you manage to eat anything?

Rita   Yes. Thank you.

Enter **Immacolata**.

Immacolata   Has she eaten anything?

Antonio   She's had a little soup – a little mozzarella . . . Take her to the kitchen and persuade her to have something else.

Immacolata (*clearing the table*)   Yes, you come with me, young lady. Come on.

Rita   No, no . . . I saved that for Rafiluccio. Do eat it, Rafiluccio. There's meat in the soup.

Rafiluccio   Thank you, I'm not hungry.

(*To* **Immacolata**.) You can take it away.

Geraldina   Eat it – if it will stop her worrying –

Rita   Please, Rafiluccio –

Rafiluccio   I'm not hungry.

Antonio   Fine. Just leave it – his appetite may come back later – but now we have things to discuss . . . So go away –

Immacolata (*to* **Rita**)   Come on.

She starts to follow **Geraldina**, *but . . .*

Rita   I'll be with you in a minute.

(*She goes to* **Rafiluccio**, *takes his hands and looks into his eyes, and after a while says:*) Rafilu', I'll go if it's what you want. Talk to Don Antonio – I know he'll show you the right thing to do. But never forget that I'm your woman. And . . . (*whispers*) eat the soup – the piece of meat . . . You've had nothing this morning.

Rafiluccio   All right –

Rita   Good!

Follows **Geraldina** *and* **Immacolata**.

Rita   Which way's the kitchen?

Geraldina   We'll show you.

Exeunt.

Antonio   She seems a determined sort of girl.

Rafiluccio   She's a saint.

Antonio   Sit down, my boy.

Rafiluccio   Thank you.

Sits.

Antonio   So?

Rafiluccio (*nervous*)   Don Anto' . . . It's just that . . . Don Anto' . . .

Antonio   Young man, I know how things are. The world turns – we must face all that life throws at us – and do whatever becomes necessary. Two hours ago you told me quite coldly – with mathematical certainty: 'I must kill my father.' Now I see you're nervous – you're holding back. In these last two hours you've thought things through, and now you find those words 'kill my father' you were so sure of –

Rafiluccio   No, Don Anto'. Forgive me for interrupting you. You're right to think I'm nervous – it's because I've heard what everybody says about you – though I've never before had the honour to come and meet you. When the name Antonio Barracano is mentioned people shut their mouths – they bow their heads. I respect that reputation – it's why I find I'm lost for words in your presence. And I think I know what you're going to say . . . But a man must be a man. What I said two hours ago still holds, and tomorrow morning –

Antonio   You'll kill your father.

Rafiluccio   It's my fate – and my misfortune. It was meant to be.

Antonio   So why have you come to me? Is it because you want my approval? Why should I care what you do? Do you think I'm your confessor? If you'd come to me and said 'Don Anto', I'm in trouble . . . these are the facts of the case and so on . . .' – I could have advised you – helped you. But you say the decision has already been made – because: 'A man must be a man.'

What I have to tell you is that a man can be a man only when he realises that he's is not infallible – when he understands that a bad decision must be reversed. When he can accept his mistakes – take responsibility for them – want to put those mistakes right . . . When he can temper bravery with caution . . . When he knows how far his courage will take him . . . When he can learn from being afraid . . . When he can admit there are better men than himself and they may have the answers he lacks. Rafiluccio, I'm the man with the answers. Either leave now . . . or prepare yourself to follow my advice.

Rafiluccio (*no longer sure of anything*)   Don Anto' . . .

Antonio (*grave*)   He's your father. You're his son. Do you know what that means? Or not?

Rafiluccio (*rebelliously, like the victim of an injustice*)   Perhaps he's the one that doesn't know what it means? When I came into this world, my father already had his place in it. When my father was born I had no say in the matter. Don Anto', Arturo Santaniello hasn't been a father to me: he's been a shit.

Antonio   That's for me to decide – that's if you want to hear what I have to say. I'll tell you if your father's a shit or not . . . And then it may turn out that it's you who's the shit.

Rafiluccio   Don Anto' . . .

Antonio   Enough! When did you last see your father?

Rafiluccio   Over a year ago.

Antonio   Did you part on bad terms?

Rafiluccio   The worst. He said: 'You're no son of mine. Get yourself a job in some other pastry shop, and never set foot in my house again.'

Antonio   So now people are running to him, carrying tales: 'Your son's been saying this or that terrible thing about you', and others are telling you your father's been saying this or that terrible thing about you? You've never spoken to him since?

Rafiluccio   No.

Antonio   What sort of schooling did he give you?

Rafiluccio (*ashamed*)   Very little. Primary school – then my father said that it would be better if I started earning a living so he put me to work in his shop. But I can read and write.

Antonio   I can't. (*Laughs.*) Well, I read a little but I can't write. I can manage the newspaper – especially the headlines – the big letters. Anything handwritten has to be read out to me. Anyway, you get by?

Rafiluccio   I get by.

Antonio   I get by too . . . My boy, I'm not going to ask you what's caused this rift between you and your father. They say a church always has two bells – and I only feel comfortable when I hear both bells sound together. One bell on its own means there's going to be a funeral: I don't like funerals.

Rafiluccio   Don Anto', may I say something?

Antonio   Of course. It's what you're here for.

Rafiluccio   When you speak, people listen. I think my father would listen to you if you warned him what I'm intending to do. Unless he gives me what's due to a son –

Antonio   First I'd have to hear his side of the story. Do you have a gun?

Rafiluccio (*after a brief pause*)   Yes, sir.

Antonio   On you?

Rafiluccio   Yes.

Antonio   Put it on the table.

Rafiluccio   Here.

Antonio   That's all?

Rafiluccio   That's all.

Enter **Amedeo**.

Amedeo   I'm back, Papa. I've done what you wanted.

(*To* **Rafiluccio**.) Hello.

Rafiluccio   Hello.

Antonio   And?

Amedeo   He's outside. Will you see him now?

Antonio   Wait.

Immacolata *has followed* **Amedeo** *in*.

Antonio   'Macula, there's somebody to see me. Give me a minute then fetch him in.

Immacolata   Right!

Exit.

Antonio   My boy, there's something I must do at once. Amedeo will go with you.

Amedeo   We'll wait in my room. Come on.

Rafiluccio (*frustrated*)   But . . . will you call –

Antonio   I'll call you.

The young men go out. **Immacolata** *brings in* **Arturo Santaniello**.

Immacolata   Come in. Here's Don Antonio –

Arturo   Thanks –

He's about sixty, still handsome, of peasant stock. He stares a lot – the habit of stubborn, difficult people. Well dressed in a quiet suit.

Antonio   Ah. You're Santaniello – Arturo Santaniello?

Arturo   Don Antonio.

Small bow.

Antonio   Thank you for coming to see me.

Arturo (*looking out of the window, admiring the estate*) Your land? All of it?

Antonio   You can't see it all from here – four kilometres up to the olive grove – as far again to the left, and over there it stretches all the way to the sea. Yes, it's all mine.

Arturo   Lucky man.

Antonio   Forty years ago, when I came back from America . . . I bought it then.

Arturo   Land was cheap in those days.

Antonio   Dirt cheap. Then I started to build a few properties – villas – just a few –

Arturo   A little paradise. But the architects – the engineers – they're not cheap –

Antonio   Ha! Get involved with architects and engineers and you're on the way to beggary. I do it all myself. There's an old builder I've used for years – my daughter looks after the paperwork and purchasing: cement, stone, bricks, scaffolding, plaster –

Arturo   What about planning permission?

Antonio   Out here? It's just more paperwork, isn't it?

Arturo   So you don't bother?

Antonio   What was the greatest invention man ever made? Not the radio – television – not the atom bomb – space travel? – No, Don Arturo, nobody has ever come up with a greater invention than paper.

Arturo (*amused*)   Really?

Antonio   What can you do with paper?

Arturo   Well –

Antonio   You can make proposals, agreements, contracts, books, newspaper . . . And banknotes . . .

Arturo   Ah yes. Money.

Antonio   And something else. What do you think is the most important use for paper? The most important of all?

Arturo   You tell me. I've no idea.

Antonio   There was once a man – a man of genius – we don't know his name – who took a piece of brown paper, cut it into a small square, folded down the four corners, coated the edges with gum, stuck down three of the sides, but left the fourth open. The fourth side is allowed to dry. It only becomes sticky again if you get a little spit on your tongue and run it along that fourth edge.

Arturo   An envelope?

Antonio   Now an envelope really comes into its own if you stuff it full of banknotes – also made of paper – and seal it up. Forget architects and engineers – forget planning permission! I tell you, Don Arturo, without that sealed envelope I'd be finished. There are wicked people in this world who go about to trap some poor idiot who fondly imagines he can put up a building – a poor idiot who know all the rules and regulations by heart, and who doesn't understand the power of paper – the hypnotic effect of the brown envelope – and they never leave him alone until he's in the bankruptcy court or the lunatic asylum. Some people worry because they are taught: 'The law doesn't recognise ignorance of the law as a defence in law.' It's not true! Believe me, Don Arturo, the law doesn't recognise three-quarters of the population. What the law *does* recognise is a brown paper envelope stuffed with banknotes. Then the law is happy to keep itself in ignorance.

Arturo   I remember you as a young man, many years ago.

Antonio   When I was living in America?

Arturo   I've never been there. No . . . In Naples . . . forty years ago. You were up in court.

Antonio   Ah. You followed my case.

Arturo   Didn't everybody? It was a very famous trial. In those days I was fascinated by all that – in the newspapers – gangster killings. Hadn't you killed a –

Antonio   I was eighteen when it happened.

Arturo   And then you disappeared –

Antonio   With the help of somebody I knew in America – he's still alive – eighty-three years old – we still keep in touch –

Arturo   What's his name?

Antonio   Perhaps you ask too many questions. With his help I was smuggled on board a ship bound for the States.

The court condemned me 'in absentia'. I was out there for seventeen years. This man I spoke of looked after me – helped me make my way – I worked for him. At what, you'll ask?

Arturo *suspects something criminal as we see by his expression.*

Nothing dishonourable. Bloodshed was involved, naturally, but always in a just cause. The dollars I saved – not exactly riches in America – but back here in Naples – with exchange rates as they were after the war . . . Well, I made my fortune. I came home, bought land, gave myself up to the authorities and demanded a re-trial. Council for my defence was De Fonzeca – new evidence was raked up, for and against me. Eight witnesses swore I'd acted in self-defence. So I got off.

Arturo   Your witnesses told the truth?

Antonio   No. They lied through their teeth. But in a just cause.

Arturo   Ah . . . and De Fonzeca – your lawyer? Was he corrupt too?

Antonio   If you want to win your case my rule is: tell your lawyers nothing. My witnesses lied, but not me – I told the truth. I said what happened. I had right on my side. I have two fractured ribs. My lower jaw is riveted together with a metal plate . . . All down to the watchman – Giacchino . . . What a shit he was! Good riddance. I killed him . . . a shit. I was only eighteen . . .

I looked after the goats . . . I started life among the goats. This watchman – Giacchino took a dislike to me – who knows why? – I'd say to him: 'Giacchi' you let everybody else graze their goats on this land – why not me?' And he'd raise his gun – like this – and say: 'I'm here just to keep you out. It's OK for the others, but for you . . . No. Get lost or I'll shoot you.' One morning, I'd eaten a little bread – a little cheese – the goats were cropping the grass nearby – I suppose some of them must have wandered into Giacchino's fields . . .

And suddenly blows are raining down on me – I woke up –
blows, slaps, kicks all over my body – I couldn't think if it was
a nightmare or if it was really happening – but I can hear
Giacchino's voice saying: 'Now perhaps you won't forget
who's watchman here . . .' Don Arturo, my own mother
wouldn't have recognised me – my face was just blood and
filth. I didn't tell the hospital what happened – said I'd fallen
down the mountain . . .

Don Arturo, day after day, week after week, I was burning
up inside. I'd walk down the street . . . and see Giacchino.
Everywhere. Did I see my friends? Only Giacchino. At
my bedside, every night: Giacchino! It was like electric. I
thought to myself: if I don't kill Giacchino I won't survive. I
must kill him . . . I must kill him . . . he must die – he must
or I will.

(*In a trance.*) Me or Giacchino . . . Me or Giacchino . . . Me
or Giacchino . . . Don Arturo, I bought myself a knife. I
went back to the place where he worked. As watchman . . .
'Hey, Giacchi!' He never got a chance to point his gun – 'I'm
coming to get you!' 'It wasn't me, I never touched you!' 'It
wasn't you?' 'No!' 'You swear?' ' I swear to you!' 'You swear
on your children's life?' 'I swear on my children's life!'
'Honest to God?' 'Honest to God!' Then I stabbed him. If
he hadn't lied I might have let him off. It was fifty-seven
years ago. I haven't finished with Giacchino yet, Don Arturo
. . . I just keep on . . . stabbing him . . . stabbing, stabbing,
stabbing . . .

Arturo   Forgive me, Don Antonio. In my opinion you
should have gone to the proper authorities –

Antonio   So he could have denied it?

Arturo   Even so –

Antonio   Who were my witnesses: him, me and the goats?
And the goats would have kept their mouths shut. Put him
in the dock and he'd perjure himself before God. There are
two types of men – the honest men and the shits. Giacchino

was a prince among the shits. The honest men can't bend the law. The penal code has 266 pages and 734 articles. Giacchino – what does he say to that? He says 'Tell me which law you're charging me under and I'll tell you a way round it.' So what can the judge do? This is the law, this is the evidence, and these are the witnesses' sworn statements. Even if it's obvious that the accused is innocent – that the accuser is lying – a judge can't think like an ordinary man. All he can do is apply the rules. Like a proof in mathematics. We can't blame the law. Blame the shits that work the system. It's the ignorant who must suffer. I'm here to look after the ignorant.

Arturo (*thinks he's mad; unsettled; smiles*)   Ah well . . .

Antonio   But that's not why we're here – I've wandered off the point and I'm wasting your time.

Arturo   Not at all.

Antonio   I'm speaking in confidence. If it hadn't been just the two of us I'd have kept my mouth shut. About . . .

Arturo   I understand.

Antonio   Don Arturo, I've put you to this trouble, because I'm going to ask a personal favour of you. Also because I wish to offer you my assistance – It's an unpleasant affair which pleases none of us. But there's a simple solution – no sane or honest man keeps open a wound when there's an easy remedy at hand –

Arturo   Just say the word. Anything I can do to help –

Antonio   You're too kind. Then . . . I hear there's bad blood between you and your son.

Arturo   I don't have a son.

Antonio   Don Arturo, don't play games with me. You're a man so answer like a man. You have a son: Rafiluccio.

Arturo   Had! Had a son! – Rafiluccio. I'd forgotten his name until you reminded me.

Antonio   That's bad. This – er – breakdown –

Arturo   Don Anto', I was twelve years old when I started baking bread. Through hard work – personal sacrifice – and, I thank God, natural ability – today I have two thriving businesses. And here I am – still hard at work; every morning I'm up by five. While he . . . he's spineless, gutless, immoral – and ungrateful. I tried hard to make a son of him – it was a waste of time. 'Let's stay in tonight,' I say, ' keep me company – watch television – we'll play cards.' No sir! Always some excuse: 'There's someone I must see – why didn't you mention it this morning?' He treats his friends better than his father –

Antonio   He's young – The young need people of their own age –

Arturo   'Hey, Rafilu',' I'd say: 'Tomorrow's the last day for getting our tax returns in – I hope you've not forgotten?' ''Course I've not forgotten!' Three days later he's still not even started to fill in the forms . . . It never stops . . . There's another thing: I like a bit of salt cod on Fridays. 'Rafilu',' I say, 'have you soaked the cod?' ''Course I have!' he says. I get home Friday evening – has he soaked my cod? Has he hell! He's out with his mates. I'd call that ingratitude, wouldn't you? I've got this big portrait of my wife – photograph – nice frame – it matches the one of myself that hangs in the bakery: after Friday mass I always put flowers, candles – light the little lamps in front of it – it's something devout I like to do. 'Hey, Rafilu' – tomorrow I'll need more candles.' Tomorrow comes – no candles. I'm wasting my breath. Those candles keep alive the memory of his mother – Does he care? No he doesn't – and when I bid this world goodnight and I'm up there with her do you think my portrait will get any candles? No – none for his mother and none for me either. He won't try – he just won't make the effort. By nature I'm a worker – by nature he's a sponger:

we're never going to agree about anything. And then – as I've said – all that ingratitude . . .

Antonio   But if you helped him get started –

Arturo   Ah, now we're getting to it – If I set him up in business –

Antonio   After all he's not a rival – he's your son. But you think it would look as if you were trying to buy his affection?

Arturo   Exactly. What else would it be?

Antonio   I understand that. But that's the way it's always been? Don Arturo, my friend, children are a gift – a gift from God – but we spend our lives paying for them.

Arturo   I'm closing the account.

Antonio   But you own two profitable businesses –

Arturo   If we're talking about the patisserie in the via Roma – You don't think I'd let him anywhere near it? It's a smart area – Anyway I don't employ men – behind the counter it's all girls – sky-blue uniforms, white caps – via Roma – you need to make a big impression . . . and there's a Swiss lady in charge of everything . . . looks after my accounts. At Giacinto Albino – well, that's where I am and where I am he can never be. And then . . . I'm master in my own house, and with all due respect to Don Antonio Barracano I will remain master. So I don't intend to discuss it any further. One thing I will say: this isn't a public dispute; it's a disagreement between father and son. And if my son has been coming to you – asking you to sort things out for him – I'd ask you to remember that this isn't about settling a row between a couple of gangsters – it's a family matter. So you just think about it.

Antonio   Now wait a minute . . . Your son didn't come here to . . . The reason the boy turned to me . . . It's something else. I'm not free to talk about it.

Arturo   I'll ask you again not to involve yourself. It's not a free for all, it's private. I've no wish to offend you, Don Anto' –

Antonio   I'm sure you've not –

Arturo   But I'm master in my own house.

With a burst of anger.

It's my money! Rafiluccio can go to hell!

Antonio   So it would seem . . . Yes, I can see you're the master.

There's a long pause; **Antonio** *is trying to think of a way to get the discussion going again.*

You have a fine gold chain . . .

Arturo   I bought it many years ago. An auction at the Banco di Napoli.

Antonio   And the locket?

Arturo   No. I bought that later – when my wife died. I keep her picture in it.

Antonio   We never stop do we? – forever buying things – acquiring things . . . Furniture, clothes, possessions –

Arturo   Until we find we own a house full of junk –

Antonio   Me too . . . I'm just the same.

Arturo   But I've stopped. I've conquered all my acquisitive urges.

Antonio   Good for you. There came a time when I stopped too. After the court quashed my sentence I got married. Then the children came along . . . spend, spend, spend. Armida said to me: 'Anto', that's enough, now! We've done OK. We've nowhere to put any more . . . Stuff!' My son Gennaro was eight. One morning he said to me: 'Papa, is it

true that when you're dead and buried this land and all this
stuff will be mine?'

Arturo   Little monkey! At eight!

Antonio   It's the way things are: aren't all children
just waiting for their fathers to die? Gennaro, Amedeo,
Geraldina . . . I thought: will they grow up just waiting for
me to die? 'No, Gennarino, my son,' I said: 'You don't have
to wait until I'm dead and buried; it's all yours now.' I sent
for a lawyer, divided everything into three parts, and made
the whole lot over to my children there and then. Now when
they call me 'Papa' I feel – and they feel too – what the word
truly means. Would you just give me a moment?

Arturo   Help yourself.

Antonio *goes and brings in* **Rafiluccio**. *At first the boy doesn't
notice his father and the father does not notice his son. Then*
Rafiluccio *sees* **Arturo** *and freezes. There's a similar reaction from*
Arturo. *With contempt.*

Arturo   So you've come here hoping Don Anto' will do your
dirty work –

Antonio   That's not why he came –

Rafiluccio   I'm here on other business.

Arturo   Then it's no business of mine. So why involve me?

Antonio   You can't help being involved – it's an explosive
situation.

Arturo   Don Anto', I don't know what's been going on. I do
know this little crawler's wasting my time – and yours. He
and I have severed all connections and he'd better not forget
it – I've forbidden him my home, my shops – both him and
his whore.

Rafiluccio *(fury)*   You're the one who keeps a whore! The
biggest fattest tart in the whole pastry shop –

Arturo   Good day, Don Antonio –

Heads for the door.

Amedeo *comes in followed by* **Rita**.

Rafiluccio   I mean the whore in our home, the whore in our shops – the whore with her fingers in the till – the Swiss whore – the Swiss cow –

Amedeo   What's going on?

Rafiluccio   I can't get a job! – everywhere I go they slam the door in my face – 'Why'd your father sack you?' – the lies you tell about me – to cover up the fact you'd no reason – no right to sack me! – But your whore's got it all now – whatever she wants – anything –

Arturo   It's my money! Mine! In my house I'll do as I like – have who I like – are you listening to me! Never let me set eyes on you again! – My house – via Giacinto Albino – forget they exist!

(*With fury.*) Keep away from me! *You* don't exist!

Rafiluccio   Shut your filthy mouth! My God!

Grips a chair and would attack **Arturo** *but* **Amedeo** *stops him.*

Rita (*holding onto* **Rafiluccio**)   Rafilu', for the love of God! Don't do this!

Arturo   Oh, she's here as well – the doting fiancée – I see she's more of my happy family up the spout –

Rafiluccio (*trying to get at him*)   Mother of God!

Armida *comes in.*

Armida   Anto', what's wrong?

Antonio   Nothing. Nothing at all –

Arturo (*to* **Rafiluccio**)   You're pathetic! What could you ever hope to achieve but failure?

(*To the others.*) Look at him . . . this . . . to his father. You see what he is?

(*To* **Rafiluccio**.) You sicken me! Keep away, d'y' hear! Don Anto', I'm sorry I can't bring myself to do as you ask. In other circumstances, perhaps . . . I see why he's come running to you – that's fine – do what you have to . . . But I'm warning you – stop meddling in my family's affairs.

Antonio   Warning *me*? You threaten me? I'm not sure I like your tone. I'm not sure I ever liked it –

Arturo   Well, if you don't like it, Don Antonio Barracano . . . you can always lump it.

Antonio   Shut your mouth! When I'm talking . . . you shut your mouth . . . You haven't listened to a word I've said. And if you're not careful you'll make an enemy of me.

Armida   Holy mother of God!

Horrified; she signals to **Amedeo** *who goes out.*

Antonio   Nobody says to me 'Stop meddling' – and nobody has ever dared tell me to 'lump it'.

Arturo   Well, maybe you've never stuck your nose into private, family matters before?

Antonio   I feed you good counsel and you bite my hand. You'd have done well to remember who I am. I'm Don Antonio Barracano.

Arturo   Sure you are! And I'm an honest man – I work for what I have – I respect the law, and my name's Arturo Santaniello.

Antonio (*with gravity, producing his gun*)   Do you carry a gun?

Arturo   No, Don Anto' –

Enter **Geraldina** *and* **Immacolata**.

Geraldina   Papa –

Arturo   I don't play with guns.

Amedeo *and* **Fabio** *come in and look at the two men apprehensively.*

Arturo   Don Antonio Barracano shouldn't need me to remind him what an honourable and courageous thing it is to threaten an unarmed man.

Antonio (*calmly indicates* **Rafiluccio**'s *revolver on the table and invites* **Arturo** *to take it up.* **Arturo** *refuses.* **Antonio** *puts his own gun on the table*)   You're not a man. You're beneath contempt –

Arturo   Coming from such as you . . . Who could presume to argue with your judgement –

Antonio   A filthy little sh – sh – shopkeeper!

Arturo   I note your comments and will try to do better in the future –

Antonio   Scum –

Arturo   I'm honoured. And sorry that my filthy presence has, for a moment, soiled your lovely home. Thank you for your hospitality and for the wise counsel you've freely offered me. So a trial can be rigged can it? But not all trials. Let me tell you there are cases where justice must prevail. There is some evidence even you can't tamper with – and there are witnesses – a few men you can't buy. A little patience is what I need; what you need is a little more humility, a little more common sense.

(*To them all.*) Good day.

Exits.

Antonio   That! A man?

Rafiluccio   Mother of God! Why did I let him –

Antonio   But he's still your father! That gives him a power over you. He understands exactly what that power means and you don't . . . It's a life sentence! Do you know what I'm saying?

Armida (*very frightened*)   But what is it –

Fabio   A life sentence?

Amedeo   Papa?

Rita   Do nothing, Rafilu' –

Imploring.

Think of us – Why ruin all our lives?

Rafiluccio   Don Anto', help me!

Antonio   He's your father.

Rafiluccio   My father! But what does that *mean*!

Antonio   Rafiluccio, let me explain it . . . You too, Doctor – listen – and Amedeo – everybody listen to me. If Antonio Barracano decides to help you, the next big event in Arturo Santaniello's life could be his own funeral. I'll tell you how it might be done. You walk past the shop in Giacinto Albino – stop – check he's there – you go in – put four bullets in his head – that should do it – and with the fifth – you turn round and shoot out the shop window. So what's the story? Whose gun was it? It belonged to your father. He fired the first shot as you walked through the door – the shot that smashed the window – you tried to disarm him, grabbed the gun, there was a struggle, and the rest . . . What sort of a man was he? Clearly he hated you: abusive behaviour, his son thrown out on the street, he consorts with a prostitute. The jury will say self-defence. There will be witnesses to swear it was. You'll be cleared completely or let off with a warning . . . 'Don't do it again . . .'

Rafiluccio   But . . .

Antonio   But – Mother of God! – he gave you life. When your rage dies – when the madness leaves you – you will have killed the man who once loved you more than his own life. Could you go on living?

Immacolata   Think again – you're young – you've your whole life ahead of you –

Armida   Ask Our Lady to help you – think of your baby son – Our Lady won't abandon you now there are children to think of –

Rita   Our Lady would get you a driving job – he's a brilliant driver – and once he's passed his test –

Amedeo   *We*'ll find you a job – if that's all! – We'll help you – me, Gennaro, Papa –

They all make encouraging noises – all want to comfort and help him – all want him to change his mind about killing **Arturo**.

Antonio   Think very carefully, Rafilu'. And remember what I said to you a while ago: 'A man is only a man when he accepts he's not infallible – when he accepts that a bad decision must be reversed.'

Rafiluccio (*makes a genuine attempt but despairs of changing his mind*)   I can't do it! Don Anto', I'm not to blame – believe me! – When I think of that man – I can't even say the word 'father'! – Look at me! Look at my hands! I can't stop shaking. This one thought possesses me, I can't sleep at night – I can't eat, can't sleep, can't speak – a single thought – I'm possessed!

Beating his head.

Stop tormenting me! For God's sake stop tormenting me! I can't escape it, Don Anto' – if a friend speaks to me it's Papa's voice I hear. I close my eyes – it's his face see – his face – Every night he's at my bedside . . . Don Anto', look what it's doing to me – in two months I've lost so much weight . . . I can't go on! I can't go on – it's burning me up – my life – I don't want to die – I'm a young man – why should I want to die! – It's him or me – it has to be one of us –

Sinks trembling into a chair and buries his face in his hands.

Antonio   I know, I know . . .

Thinking of Giacchino he is, for once, lost for the right words to say to **Rafiluccio**.

Antonio   Poor boy. You're in the grip of a terrible fever. We catch it from the earth we tread on. It worms its way through the soles of our shoes, up through the flesh, into the bone, eating – eating it's way, at last, into our brains. Once in the brain it begins to whisper to us – kill, kill, kill! It tells us where we should strike, the best time, the weapon we should strike with – and then the fever leaves us. And we face a lifetime rotting in jail.

You came to me – your counsellor. So you must leave everything in my hands. At your age I killed Giacchino. This is something different – Arturo Santaniello is your father. He must be given a warning. He must be made to see why you had to come to me – and he must be told why I've decided to intervene. 'Macula – fetch my hat and stick.

Immacolata   Right.

She gets them.

Antonio   This is how it works. When there's something you want you go to the owner and make him an offer. Then you wait. Now there is something I want of Arturo Santaniello. So I'm going to make him an offer. We'll wait and see what he does. Then I'll make my decision. First he'll have his say . . . and then I'll have mine. Doctor, I must drive into Naples. Will you come with me?

Fabio   Of course. I'll drive.

Act Three

Sun setting. **Don Antonio**'s *splendid house in Naples. There is clearly something wrong with* **Don Antonio**, *who looks pale and drained and sits oddly.* **Fabio** *finishes a letter and takes the sheet from the typewriter.*

Fabio   It needs your signature.

Antonio   Read out what I dictated first. There may be something you forgot.

Fabio   I've written exactly what you told me to write. We've no time to lose. In any sense . . .

Takes the sheet out of the machine.

Listen carefully.

Doorbell rings.

That's Luigi.

He lets in **Luigi** *and* **Vicenza**.

Fabio   Excellent! Well done, Luigi. And thanks, Vicenzella.

Luigi   I think I've got everything. Eight roast chicken like you said – salad, cheese and cake – 'cept she said it wasn't a cake it was a gateau.

Fabio   Take it into the kitchen. Put the chicken on the big serving dishes.

Vicenza (*has a basket of salad, fruit and ice*)   I'll put the fruit on ice and wash the salad – it can be dressed at the table.

Fabio   You'll have to hurry.

Luigi   Hey, Doctor, they wouldn't believe me at the cake shop when I said the order was for Don Antonio: 'Don Antonio,' they said, 'nonsense! He's still in Terzigno with his family.' They just wouldn't have it. 'He's here,' I said, 'back here in Naples.' 'We're just into September,' they said. 'He never comes back before the middle of October.'

Fabio It's only for the night. We'll go back to Terzigno in the morning.

Luigi Well, come home soon, Don Anto' . . . business is always bad when you take a holiday.

Moves towards kitchen.

Get a move on, Vicenza.

Vicenza Excuse me.

They exit to kitchen.

Fabio How are you feeling?

Antonio Oddly enough, Doctor, I feel nothing.

Fabio It's not possible. The blade went in about six centimetres. I don't have my instruments with me – no surgical knives, no iodine – there's nothing more I can do. I've bandaged you up as best I can . . . You're lucky to be still alive, but . . . .. 'I'm not feeling too well,' he says . . . You should have told me the truth straight away. I'd have driven you straight to casualty –

Antonio Where I'd have had to answer endless questions. Fill in forms – name names – do I want to press charges? Is it likely? Because for once I'm the man with the problem? You know how many disputes and crimes I have settled – and always in my own way. Now something's happened to me: 'Please, sirs, I want him punished.' Never.

Fabio You could have said you didn't know your attacker: 'a person or persons unknown – I might recognise him if I saw him again.' You know how it works.

Antonio And what about my family? My sons? Gennaro and Amedeo knew I was going to talk to Arturo Santaniello . . . it wouldn't take them long to find out the truth. They'd go after him. More bloodshed, yet another vendetta. It's enough, Doctor . . . Enough is enough. For thirty-five years you and I have worked together – done all we could to staunch the flow of blood . . . would you have me add to it?

Fabio   But didn't he give you chance to say why you were there?

Antonio   No. I walked in the shop and he stabbed me . . . The silly bastard must have thought I'd come to shoot him . . . I said: 'Don Arturo, I need to talk to you.' 'Come in,' he said – nobody in the shop – I moved towards him . . . Either he had the knife in his hand, or it was lying behind the counter – I don't know. But the fact is he stabbed me. Here. (*Indicates left side of his abdomen.*) And just as it happened a customer walks in. Funny. Like a farce. Can you guess who it was? Vicienzo Cuozzo. The fellow who was with me this morning, the one who called me . . .

Fabio   What? The one who kept shouting 'Don Anto is our father – Don Anto' is everybody's father – Let's fall down and worship Don Antonio!' I heard him all the way up the street. Didn't he try to help you?

Antonio   No. He just ran off and left me there – in a pool of my own blood. (*Thinks.*) Do you know who our biggest danger is now? Vicienzo Cuozzo. If he shoots his mouth off, my sons will kill Santaniello and spend the rest of their lives in jail.

Fabio   Well, what can we do? I'm afraid that's the way it works.

Antonio   Not if I can stop it.

Fabio   How can you?

Antonio   Have you done what I asked?

Fabio   I've done everything you asked me to. Everybody has been invited, I've made arrangements to deal with Arturo Santaniello and I went to see Cuozzo in his workshop. He swears he'll be here.

Antonio Then let this be your farewell dinner. I mean it.
So farewell. The day after tomorrow you can go. There'll be
no problems. Enjoy your new life in America.

Short pause.

I can honestly say . . . I feel nothing.

Feels his forehead.

A little perspiration . . . Will you get me some water?

Fabio You see? I told you. You're starting to feel thirsty.

Gives him some water.

Because your peritoneum is burst and your spleen is
ruptured.

Antonio Fascinating. Would you just read the letter,
please?

Fabio 'Dear Bastiano . . . the person who brings you this
letter is Doctor Fabio Della Ragione who has been with me
for many years. As well as being my doctor he has made
great sacrifices for the common cause and been a loyal
helper. He has come to America to join his brother because
he's tired and reached that stage in life when he deserves a
little peace and a rest. Introduce him to our friends and see
he's treated with the same respect they would extend to me.
He will tell you how I am and answer any questions you put
to me. I'm not long for this world. Don't let it upset you, it
doesn't upset me. I've lived seventy-five full years and I've
done pretty well for myself. If I had it all to do again I'd
do it, and I'd do it in the same way, including Giacchino.
This may be the last time I write to you. I kiss your hand
in gratitude for everything you've done for me since I was
eighteen years old. Look after yourself and remember me to
all our friends. Your most affectionate . . .' Is that OK?

Antonio Give me the pen.

Fabio *gives him a pen and he signs.*

Antonio   Antonio Barracano.

Takes a ring off his finger and gives it to **Fabio**.

Antonio   This is for you . . .

Fabio (*deeply moved*)   Don Anto' . . .

Antonio   See if it fits.

Fabio (*puts it on*)   Yes. It does.

Antonio   Bastiano gave it to me when I came back to Italy.
He said: 'It must only be taken from your finger, by a close
friend, when you have closed your eyes for the last time.
This person must bring it back to me if I'm still living; if
I'm not let him keep it.' It's the ring given to Bastiano by
his father – a good man who was falsely accused and died in
prison. It's a long story. Show him the ring and he'll raise his
hat. If he's not wearing a hat he'll go and put one on, come
back and raise his hat to the ring. Get me a drink.

Fabio *gives him more water*.

Antonio   Terrible thirst . . . Ruptured spleen, you know
. . . (*Drinks*.) It happened – what? – an hour ago? Will I last
another hour?

Fabio   Yes.

Antonio   Tomorrow you must go back to Terzigno. It's the
dogs – Munaciello and Malavita . . . I won't let them suffer.
My family isn't always willing to see the best side of the poor
creatures. Do it with your syringe . . .

Makes the gesture of sending somebody to the next world.

Fabio   Don't worry.

Antonio   This suit, and the shirt . . . silk – first time on.
Ruined. I'll not be wearing them again. We can't send them
to the cleaners. I'll have to change. Nobody must see me
in these clothes . . . tomorrow morning . . . Put these in a
suitcase and get rid of them. Have you filled out my death
certificate?

Fabio   There's no need –

Antonio   Is it ready?

Fabio   It will be. When the time comes.

Antonio   What will you put?

Fabio   Whatever you like.

Antonio   Heart attack. A massive heart attack. That should do it.

Fabio   Fine. (*Doorbell rings.*) Who's that?

Vicenza (*entering*)   I'll get it.

Fabio   It may be Cuozzo.

Antonio   Let's hope so.

Drinks a little water.

Fabio   Don't worry. He'll be here.

Vicenza   Come in. Don Antonio.

She brings in **Rafiluccio** *and* **Rita**, *before returning to the kitchen.*

Rafiluccio   Good evening, Don Anto'.

Rita   Good evening.

Antonio   Is it?

Rafiluccio   Don Anto', I had to see you but I didn't know where you were. It was lucky I met Vicienzo Cuozzo who said he knew you were here in Naples for the evening because you'd asked him to dinner –

Antonio   Well, here I am.

Rafiluccio   Your wife, Donna Armida, has been like a saint to us. I can't tell you how very kind . . . I was so moved . . . she spoke as if she were my mother –

Rita   She says there's an apartment with two rooms and a kitchen we can have –

Rafiluccio   And she's grown so fond of Rita – she said 'Wait until you're settled – before you start paying rent.'

Rita   And your son says Rafiluccio can work with him in his shop.

Rafiluccio   Don Anto', I've been thinking about what you said to me: 'A man can only be a man when he can accept that he's made a mistake, and he wants to put that mistake right.' I want to be a man, Don Anto'. And I've come to tell you that you need no longer concern yourself with what I'd planned to do to my father.

Rita   Our Lady has made him see sense!

Antonio (*mildly ironic*)   Well done, Our Lady! I'm delighted. And the best news is that I've already spoken to your father. His response was . . . most unexpected.

Rafiluccio   Ah?

Rita   What did he say?

Antonio   Oh, he was very reasonable in the end. He'd had time to think things over you see. He said: 'How can I refuse you anything, Don Anto'? Just tell me how much money I should make over to my son.' I suggested two million lire. Well, he wasn't too keen at first – tried to knock me down – but in the end he had to give in. He got the point.

Rafiluccio   Is this true?

Antonio   Yes. Naturally he couldn't put his hands on so much cash right away. I said: 'All right, Don Arturo . . . I'll pay the boy, and you can pay me back when you have the money.' We're both gentlemen, we shook hands on it. That's all it took. I'll give you the two million now, if that's all right with you, and I'll settle up with your father later. Doctor, my wallet's in my jacket pocket – would you be so kind? I've a severe pain in my left arm . . . I can't seem to move it.

Fabio   I'll get it.

Takes out the wallet.

Antonio   My cheque book should be there.

Fabio   Here.

Antonio   You write the cheque and I'll sign it. Put: Naples, 10 September 1960.

He does.

Make it out to Rafiluccio Santaniello. Two million lire.

Fabio   There.

Antonio   Pass it over.

He does.

Here you are, Rafilu' . . . and good luck to you.

Rafiluccio   Don Anto', I don't know how I'll ever be able to repay such kindness. (*To* **Rita**.) Kiss Don Antonio's hand.

Rita   Both his hands!

She does.

Antonio   Thank you, there's no need . . . Think of me sometimes . . . And now I'm going to have to say goodbye to you both. We're expecting guests.

Rafiluccio   We must go, Rita. Don Antonio has things to do. Good evening, Doctor.

Fabio   Good evening.

Rafiluccio   And thank you again.

Rafiluccio *and* **Rita** *go out.*

Antonio   Where's that letter?

Fabio   The one to Don Bastiano?

Antonio   No, that's the one you're taking to America – where's the one you wrote first?

Fabio   Here.

Gives it to **Antonio**.

Antonio   Keep hold of it. When I ask you, hand it to me.

Enter **Vicenza**.

Vicenza   We're ready when you are, Doctor. White wine or red?

Fabio   Red wine with roast chicken.

Doorbell rings.

That's the door.

Vicenza *goes to the door*.

Fabio   How are you doing?

Antonio   Oh, never better, Doctor. Sweating a little . . . that's all.

Vicenza   Come in.

She shows in **Vicienzo Cuozzo**, *then returns to the kitchen. He's nervous and says nothing. He stops just inside the room and looks at the floor.*

Fabio   Don Antonio wasn't sure you'd come.

Vicienzo   A summons from Don Antonio – how could I refuse?

Fabio   And the matter is very serious – in fact, this may be the very last time you see Don Antonio Barracano –

Vicienzo   No! Doctor, what are you saying – Holy Mother of God!

Fabio   I needn't tell you how delicate the matter is. When was it? – about an hour ago – and as there was nobody else in the shop you were the only witness. Right? Don Anto'?

Antonio   Yes. Vicienzo came in at the 'vital' moment. Ha.

Fabio   So I'll tell you why you're here. Don Anto' knows only too well how devoted you are to him and –

Vicienzo   But I don't know – what are you saying?

Fabio I'm talking about what you witnessed in Santaniello's pastry shop in via Giacinto Albino.

Vicienzo Witnessed? No! I don't know anything!

Antonio A moment, Doctor . . . What do you mean, you don't know anything? Are you trying to tell me you didn't walk into the baker's in Giacinto Albino an hour ago? You didn't see what happened to me when I was talking to Santaniello?

Vicienzo (*lying*) No. An hour ago I was at home . . . Perhaps you've made a mistake . . .

Antonio (*bitterly*) Oh I see! You weren't there . . . You know nothing – You saw nothing. Well, that's lucky for me as it happens. I think we can relax, Doctor . . . this faithless bastard will keep his mouth shut. You walked into that shop, you stared right into my eyes and you knew perfectly well what had happened to me. And you ran away.

Fabio See? I was right all along. So much for loyalty.

Antonio You're wrong. I'll be proved right in the end. I'm done for but my work goes on. Somebody else will finish the job. We have to make sure that my children's children's children – as well as those of this bastard – will live in a world with fewer dark corners.

Fabio I can't see it happening.

Antonio Well, let's say there are things you and I will never agree on. I must get out of this suit. Will you give me a hand?

Fabio Of course.

Antonio (*to* **Vicienzo**) It's a farewell party you see. The Doctor's leaving for America, the day after tomorrow . . . Well . . . that's the excuse but you may as well know the truth . . . I'm sure you won't blab. The people that are coming this evening will tomorrow be able to say – to swear – that I was taken ill. 'But how did it happen? What happened to Don

Antonio?' 'Nothing happened. Absolutely nothing . . . He
was an old man . . . seventy-five years old . . . A massive heart
attack . . .' You'd better stay too . . . you can be one of my
witnesses. My false witnesses . . .

Exits with **Fabio**. *After a brief pause the bell goes.* **Vicenza** *comes to
answer it.*

Vicenza   Left you on your own did they?

Vicienzo *doesn't reply.* **Vicenza** *lets in* **Arturo** *who is accompanied
by two very mysterious and sinister characters –* **Peppe Ciucciu**
and **Zibacchiello** *– and then goes back to the kitchen.* **Arturo**
is terrified. **Peppe** *and* **Zibacchiello** *say nothing but they smile
enigmatically.*

Arturo (*pleading*)   But can't you tell me what it's about?
What do you want? Where have you brought me? Who is it
wants to talk to me?

Peppe   Stop worrying. We're your friends.

Arturo   But where are we? What is this place?

Zibacchiello   It's a house. Can't you see?

Peppe   The table's laid, supper is waiting, the guests are on
their way – so calm down.

Arturo (*blustering*)   I'm a grown man! Not a baby to be
picked up and carried about wherever you like. (*Exasperated.*)
It's against the law! But no – an ordinary taxpayer can't go
about his lawful business these days without being set upon
by louts and hooligans! Why me? I'm just an ordinary chap
trying to earn a living? An honest living! So let me go! I don't
feel well – look –

Holds out his arms.

I'm shaking – I'm coming down with something . . . It's not
fair! I've always kept myself to myself – in my home – in
my business – I've never asked anything of anybody – first
Friday in the month I put flowers on my wife's grave – that

woman was a saint – if she were living still things would be very different I can tell you! – I'm all alone – nobody cares about me – I've a delinquent for a son – this is all his fault – Well, I hope he's satisfied – he's always made his father's life a misery – and now this! – He ruins me, my business . . . Aren't you men? Don't you have hearts? Pity? Why won't you help me!

Falls at their feet and begs.

I want to go home! Please! I kiss your hands, your feet . . . I've bought a ticket out of here . . . I'm going to Switzerland . . .

Taking out his cheque book.

Let me go – Name your price – How much do you want?

They are like stone.

Answer me, answer me! I want to go to Switzerland! Why won't you say something?

Enter **Fabio**.

Fabio   What's the matter with you for God's sake? Ah, I suppose you're Arturo Santaniello . . . Excellent . . . Everybody happy?

Arturo   I'm an honest man – I keep myself to myself –

Fabio   And that's why you're in trouble – you keep your eyes closed, you put your fingers in your ears, and you think there's nobody else on earth but you. And it's come as a great shock now that life sneaks up on you, holds you at knife's point and forces you to face the fact that all around you there are other people trying to get on with their lives! And they're all in trouble! They all need help! But it's 'I keep myself to myself – I was just minding my own business . . .' Well, I've had you brought here and, believe me, this is your business. It's definitely your business. It's business you contracted with your eyes shut and your fingers in your ears but it's all your own work. And the time's come for you to open your eyes and unplug your ears. Because it's time this business was over. (*Doorbell rings*.) Vicenzella!

She enters.

Vicenza What?

Fabio Door!

He goes out.

Vicenza Sorry.

She lets in and greets **Palummiello**, **Nait**, **Nasone** *and* **Nasone**'s **Wife**, *before returning to the kitchen.*

Vicenza Come in.

Nasone Thanks.

(*To* **Vicienzo**.) Oh, you're here too?

Vicienzo, *still crestfallen, says nothing.*

Nasone Sparkling conversationalist.

Wife Just ignore him – we all know what he is.

Nasone You're right. Waste of time.

Nait This is costing me a fortune. There's an English cruise ship just come in. But you can't say 'no' to Don Antonio Barracano –

Palummiello It's only one evening. They'll still be cruising tomorrow.

Enter **Fabio**.

Fabio Could you all come to the table?

(*Shouts*.) Vicenzella! When you're ready!

They all come to the table except **Arturo**, *who remains apart.*

Fabio Don Arturo, you're here.

Indicating a place near the middle of the table next to that left vacant for **Antonio**.

Fabio Next to me.

Peppe *and* **Zibacchiello** *fetch* **Arturo** *to the table and sit him down.*

Luigi (*bringing in the roast*)   Here's the chicken.

Vicenza (*bringing in the salad*)   And the salad.

Fabio   Come and join us. Luigi, Vicenzella – He's invited you both.

Luigi *and* **Vicenza** *sit at the table.*

Luigi (*drinking*)   Good health to us all!

Subdued conversation.

Fabio   Excuse me.

He goes. He comes back. **Antonio** *is leaning on his arm. The guests are alarmed by* **Antonio**'s *appearance. He has declined quite visibly since we last saw him. His eyes are dull – the challenge has gone out of them. He moves unsteadily and painfully. He's very pale.* **Fabio** *helps him to his place. The guests applaud in a subdued way.* **Arturo** *and* **Vicienzo** *stare down miserably at their plates.*

Antonio   Please forgive me, but I'm not feeling very well. It's just an attack of old age. Time is the enemy – he's always tracking us down – everything's fine – all's well with the world – then just when you least expect it – a stab-wound in the heart . . . I'm OK – it's nothing . . . This evening we're here to give a little send off to Doctor Fabio Della Ragione who's leaving to live in America. The Doctor has been a good friend to us all, and for many, many years – He's given up a great deal just to help us – never let any of us down – We can never repay him and we shall always be in his debt.

They all applaud the Doctor.

He wanted to remain longer among us – to stay at his post, as it were – so I had to say to him: 'Dear Doctor, there comes a time when each and every one of us must lay down his burden. I too have had my day. I'm tired, I'm failing . . .' Well, you can all see . . . I want some peace . . . to retire into

private life. So . . . From this evening Sanità – our district –
will no longer be my responsibility . . .

Peppe   Don Anto' you can't just desert us like this – without
warning – without –

Antonio   I can't go on for ever. Ignorance must find its
own way. There's a world full of people who demand help,
guidance, protection – what can one man do? In human
nature are the seeds of man's destruction. All those people
out there could learn something from the animals who have
only their own hides to look out for – unlike us – obsessed
by our possessions – our suits, shoes, shirts, ties . . . I'm
not saying that in thirty-five years all my efforts have been
futile – No! – I'd like to think I've kept a firm grip on the
prevention of crime, violence, injustice – all manner of evils
. . . We must hope that the time will come when our world
has no need of men like Don Antonio Barracano.

Nait   Stop this! You can't really want to leave us?

Antonio   It's finished. So let's make it a happy ending –
we've a good dinner here – good company . . . And also we
are pleased to welcome to our table Don Arturo Santaniello
whom I'm sure everybody knows.

Murmurs of approval and agreement.

I'm particularly pleased he could be here, and delighted to
be able to tell you all that the difficulties he's been having
with his son, Rafiluccio, have finally been settled.

Murmurs of approval.

Don Arturo was anxious to find an amicable solution –
well – his own son . . . Fortunately we were able to sort the
whole thing out for him. Don Arturo, I've done what you
asked. I've handed over the two million to Rafiluccio as you
suggested – and by the way thanks for the letter you sent me.
Er – Doctor, do we have Don Arturo's letter?

Fabio   Oh, yes –

Hands the letter he typed.

Antonio   No, you read it, Doctor – my eyesight's not what it was and . . . I'm tired.

Fabio (*reads*)   'Dear Don Antonio, I acknowledge receipt of the sum of two million lire advanced to my son, Rafiluccio. I consider it a great favour as when he needed it I found I had insufficient funds in hand. It goes without saying that I shall repay the full amount whenever you shall require it. Very many thanks, and with all good wishes, I am . . . Yours . . .'

Antonio (*takes the letter*)   Oh, look – you've forgotten to sign it. Oblige me.

Hands him the letter. **Fabio** *gives him a pen.*

Arturo (*a very faint voice*)   There.

He signs.

Antonio   Have you brought your cheque book?

Arturo   Yes.

Antonio   Make it out to Signora Armida Barracano.

Arturo *writes a cheque and gives it to* **Antonio**.

Antonio   Doctor, would you give this to my wife?

Fabio   Certainly.

Puts the cheque in his pocket.

Antonio   And now! Eat, drink, be merry . . . For . . .

Slowly his head sinks down towards the table he is still holding his right arm against his knife-wound.

All   Don Anto'! (*etc.*)

Fabio   It's nothing, it's nothing, let me deal with it. (*Helps* **Antonio** *up.*) We'd better get you to your room – you can rest for a while – I'll take a look at you . . .

Without waiting for a reply he starts helping him, slowly and painfully, out of the room.

Fabio   He'll be all right in a minute – Just carry on with – enjoy the meal.

Vicienzo *gets to his feet, tears in his eyes, and rushes over to* **Antonio**.

Vicienzo   Don Anto' . . . Oh, Don Anto' . . .

Antonio (*he can hardly get the words out*)   What is it?

Vicienzo   Don Anto' – They threatened me – made me swear to say I'd seen nothing . . .

Antonio   I know.

Moves away.

Vicienzo (*pleading*)   Don Anto' don't leave me – Say I'm forgiven . . .

Fabio   What do you –

Antonio   What more do you want from me?

Vicienzo   Your forgiveness. Wish me well.

Antonio   I wish you well.

Vicienzo   Give me your hand . . .

Antonio (*pause. Manages an ironic smile. Is just able to say*)   No. Not my hand. No . . .

Exits with **Fabio**.

Nasone   He seems unwell.

Wife   His face looks terrible.

Nait   And his age is against him.

Luigi   But he's still a strong man,

Palummiello (*to* **Nait**)   Any more wine?

Nait *passes the bottle.*

Nait   This chicken tastes like real chicken.

Nasone   I could eat a whole one.

Vicenza (*to* **Luigi**)   More salad, Papa?

They continue to eat and improvise conversation. **Fabio** *comes back, downcast. He looks at* **Antonio**'s *vacant chair and watches the guests with contempt. He studies them in turn as if he was seeing each one for the first time. He keeps on watching them. One by one they fall silent. There is a pause.*

Fabio (*in a voice which reveals nothing*)   Don Antonio is dead!

General consternation.

Nasone   Poor man!

Wife   Was it his heart?

Fabio   Was it his heart? He had a great heart. A heart which opened to anyone in need of help.

Nait   True. Men like Antonio Barracano are pretty thin on the ground.

Fabio   I worked at his side for thirty years. I admired him, loved him . . . and nobody will ever know how deeply I'm going to miss him.

Overcome with anger and emotion.

And now it's your turn to speak.

Arturo *says nothing.*

Fabio   C'mon! What have you got to say for yourself? Don Arturo?

(*To* **Vicienzo**.) What about you then?

Vicienzo *lowers his head and says nothing.*

Fabio   You had plenty to say this morning – we couldn't stop you – shouting out 'Don Antonio! Don Antonio! He's a father to us all! A father to every poor man in Naples! I'd give my life –'

Rushes to **Vicienzo** *and grabs him by the neck.*

Fabio   So what have you got to tell us!

Vicienzo   I know nothing! I tell you, I saw nothing!

Fabio   You know nothing? Don Arturo, I suppose you know nothing either? Where did we acquire this compulsion to keep sending our consciences to the laundry? Why are we all so terribly afraid of losing face? – No, it's not just us – Everybody's at it. Can any of you give me one good reason why should I go to the trouble of honouring Don Antonio's last wishes? Just to keep the likes of you from each other's throats? Eh? You haven't even got faces to save!

(*To* **Arturo** *and* **Vicienzo**.) You two – a pair of worthless cowards – scared witless at the thought of having to tell the simple truth – two loathsome lowlifes who can only deal in lies, hypocrisy, threats, blackmail . . . You'd all sleep easier in your beds, wouldn't you, if I allowed the world to think Don Anto' really had died of a massive heart attack – after spending the best years of his life trying to keep the lid on your world of petty crime – the casual violence, the cheating, the killing? His time would have been better spent fanning the flames! Well, that's exactly how I'm going to spend the few years left to me. I shan't be leaving you after all. I'm staying here.

(*Picks up telephone*.) Operator . . . Would you put a call through to a Terzigno number? The Barracano estate. I'm on 31 40 21. Thanks.

Replaces the receiver; takes the cheque for two million lire out of his pocket and throws it down in front of **Arturo**.

Fabio   Here. Take this to his widow yourself if you feel the need to start behaving like a man.

(*To* **Vicienzo**.) And you can tell the world what really happened in his shop this afternoon.

(*To the others*.) And you lot can tell everybody what really happened here tonight. I'm going to obey my conscience for once and write out Don Antonio's death certificate. And I'm actually going to tell the truth. Then Don Antonio's sons will go after Don Arturo, and both sides will call up their friends, acquaintances, relatives, allies, mercenaries and we'll have a massacre – a holocaust – total destruction. And what a good thing that will be. And it's just possible that in the ashes of this volcanic eruption we'll be able to build a new, clean world – the sort of world Don Antonio dared to dream of, with its face turned towards the sun – a world with no dark corners. So. I'm going to begin the process of truth by signing my real name on a genuine death certificate: Fabio Della Ragione. I can't tell you how much pleasure it will give me – at last! – just to be able to write the words: I certify that these are the true facts in the case . . .

He sits at the typewriter and begins to type the death certificate.

End.

Methuen Drama Student Editions

Jean Anouilh *Antigone* • John Arden *Serjeant Musgrave's Dance*
Alan Ayckbourn *Confusions* • Aphra Behn *The Rover* • Edward Bond
Lear • *Saved* • Bertolt Brecht *The Caucasian Chalk Circle* • *Fear and
Misery in the Third Reich* • *The Good Person of Szechwan* • *Life of Galileo* •
Mother Courage and her Children • *The Resistible Rise of Arturo Ui* • *The
Threepenny Opera* • Anton Chekhov *The Cherry Orchard* • *The Seagull* •
Three Sisters • *Uncle Vanya* • Caryl Churchill *Serious Money* • *Top Girls*
• Shelagh Delaney *A Taste of Honey* • Euripides *Elektra* • *Medea* •
Dario Fo *Accidental Death of an Anarchist* • Michael Frayn *Copenhagen*
• John Galsworthy *Strife* • Nikolai Gogol *The Government Inspector* •
Robert Holman *Across Oka* • Henrik Ibsen *A Doll's House* • *Ghosts* •
Hedda Gabler • Charlotte Keatley *My Mother Said I Never Should* •
Bernard Kops *Dreams of Anne Frank* • Federico García Lorca *Blood
Wedding* • *Doña Rosita the Spinster* (bilingual edition) • *The House of
Bernarda Alba* • (bilingual edition) • *Yerma* (bilingual edition) • David
Mamet *Glengarry Glen Ross* • *Oleanna* • Patrick Marber *Closer* • John
Marston *Malcontent* • Martin McDonagh *The Lieutenant of Inishmore* •
Joe Orton *Loot* • Luigi Pirandello *Six Characters in Search of an Author*
• Mark Ravenhill *Shopping and F***ing* • Willy Russell *Blood Brothers*
• *Educating Rita* • Sophocles *Antigone* • *Oedipus the King* • Wole
Soyinka *Death and the King's Horseman* • Shelagh Stephenson *The
Memory of Water* • August Strindberg *Miss Julie* • J. M. Synge *The
Playboy of the Western World* • Theatre Workshop *Oh What a Lovely
War* Timberlake Wertenbaker *Our Country's Good* • Arnold Wesker
The Merchant • Oscar Wilde *The Importance of Being Earnest* •
Tennessee Williams *A Streetcar Named Desire* • *The Glass Menagerie*

Methuen Drama Modern Plays

include work by

Edward Albee
Jean Anouilh
John Arden
Margaretta D'Arcy
Peter Barnes
Sebastian Barry
Brendan Behan
Dermot Bolger
Edward Bond
Bertolt Brecht
Howard Brenton
Anthony Burgess
Simon Burke
Jim Cartwright
Caryl Churchill
Complicite
Noël Coward
Lucinda Coxon
Sarah Daniels
Nick Darke
Nick Dear
Shelagh Delaney
David Edgar
David Eldridge
Dario Fo
Michael Frayn
John Godber
Paul Godfrey
David Greig
John Guare
Peter Handke
David Harrower
Jonathan Harvey
Iain Heggie
Declan Hughes
Terry Johnson
Sarah Kane
Charlotte Keatley
Barrie Keeffe

Howard Korder
Robert Lepage
Doug Lucie
Martin McDonagh
John McGrath
Terrence McNally
David Mamet
Patrick Marber
Arthur Miller
Mtwa, Ngema & Simon
Tom Murphy
Phyllis Nagy
Peter Nichols
Sean O'Brien
Joseph O'Connor
Joe Orton
Louise Page
Joe Penhall
Luigi Pirandello
Stephen Poliakoff
Franca Rame
Mark Ravenhill
Philip Ridley
Reginald Rose
Willy Russell
Jean-Paul Sartre
Sam Shepard
Wole Soyinka
Simon Stephens
Shelagh Stephenson
Peter Straughan
C. P. Taylor
Theatre Workshop
Sue Townsend
Judy Upton
Timberlake Wertenbaker
Roy Williams
Snoo Wilson
Victoria Wood

Methuen Drama Contemporary Dramatists

include

John Arden (two volumes)
Arden & D'Arcy
Peter Barnes (three volumes)
Sebastian Barry
Dermot Bolger
Edward Bond (eight volumes)
Howard Brenton
  (two volumes)
Richard Cameron
Jim Cartwright
Caryl Churchill (two volumes)
Sarah Daniels (two volumes)
Nick Darke
David Edgar (three volumes)
David Eldridge
Ben Elton
Dario Fo (two volumes)
Michael Frayn (three volumes)
David Greig
John Godber (four volumes)
Paul Godfrey
John Guare
Lee Hall (two volumes)
Peter Handke
Jonathan Harvey
  (two volumes)
Declan Hughes
Terry Johnson (three volumes)
Sarah Kane
Barrie Keeffe
Bernard-Marie Koltès
  (two volumes)
Franz Xaver Kroetz
David Lan
Bryony Lavery
Deborah Levy
Doug Lucie

David Mamet (four volumes)
Martin McDonagh
Duncan McLean
Anthony Minghella
  (two volumes)
Tom Murphy (six volumes)
Phyllis Nagy
Anthony Neilsen (two volumes)
Philip Osment
Gary Owen
Louise Page
Stewart Parker (two volumes)
Joe Penhall (two volumes)
Stephen Poliakoff
  (three volumes)
David Rabe (two volumes)
Mark Ravenhill (two volumes)
Christina Reid
Philip Ridley
Willy Russell
Eric-Emmanuel Schmitt
Ntozake Shange
Sam Shepard (two volumes)
Wole Soyinka (two volumes)
Simon Stephens (two volumes)
Shelagh Stephenson
David Storey (three volumes)
Sue Townsend
Judy Upton
Michel Vinaver
  (two volumes)
Arnold Wesker (two volumes)
Michael Wilcox
Roy Williams (three volumes)
Snoo Wilson (two volumes)
David Wood (two volumes)
Victoria Wood

Methuen Drama World Classics

include

Jean Anouilh (two volumes)
Brendan Behan
Aphra Behn
Bertolt Brecht (eight volumes)
Büchner
Bulgakov
Calderón
Čapek
Anton Chekhov
Noël Coward (eight volumes)
Feydeau (two volumes)
Eduardo De Filippo
Max Frisch
John Galsworthy
Gogol
Gorky (two volumes)
Harley Granville Barker
    (two volumes)
Victor Hugo
Henrik Ibsen (six volumes)
Jarry

Lorca (three volumes)
Marivaux
Mustapha Matura
David Mercer (two volumes)
Arthur Miller (six volumes)
Molière
Musset
Peter Nichols (two volumes)
Joe Orton
A. W. Pinero
Luigi Pirandello
Terence Rattigan
    (two volumes)
W. Somerset Maugham
    (two volumes)
August Strindberg
    (three volumes)
J. M. Synge
Ramón del Valle-Inclán
Frank Wedekind
Oscar Wilde

For a complete catalogue
of Methuen Drama titles
write to:

Methuen Drama
Bloomsbury Publishing Plc
36 Soho Square
London W1D 3QY

or you can visit our website at:

www.methuendrama.com